USS PRINCETON

CV/CVL-23
CV/CVA/CVS-37
LPH-5

TURNER PUBLISHING COMPANY

Turner
PUBLISHING COMPANY

Turner Publishing Company

Copyright © 2003
Publishing Rights: Turner Publishing Company
This book or any part thereof may not be
reproduced without the written consent of
Turner Publishing Company.

Library of Congress Control No. 2002117473
ISBN: 978-1-56311-862-3

Limited Edition

Contents

History of the USS Princeton 5

Stories from the USS Princeton 17

Biographies of the USS Princeton 69

Index 95

Captain's Inspection at Apra Harbor, Guam, 15 February 1947. Courtesy of James C. Creek.

HISTORY
OF THE
USS
PRINCETON

CV/CVL-23
CV/CVA/CVS-37
LPH-5

Historical Overview

The name Princeton has served has U.S. Navy well for nearly 160 years. In 1843, a sloop of war was commissioned with her name, the first Navy vessel to be powered by a steam-driven screw. The ship was decommissioned in 1849.

In 1852 the second Princeton was commissioned, and this armed transport training ship remained in service until 1866. Commissioned in 1898, the third vessel, named for the Battle of Princeton, was a composite gunboat. She served in the far east and off Nicaragua, and was decommissioned in 1919.

CV/CVL-23

The fourth *Princeton* was laid down as *Tallahassee* (CL-61) by the New York Shipbuilding Corp. in Camden, N.J., on 2 June 1941. She was reclassified CV-23 on 16 February 1942 and renamed *Princeton* 31 March 1942. Sponsored by Mrs. Harold Dodds, she was launched on 18 October 1942 and commissioned at Philadelphia 25 February 1943, with Capt. George R. Henderson in command.

Following shakedown in the Caribbean, and reclassification to CVL-23 on 15 July 1943, *Princeton*, with Air Group 23 embarked, got underway for the Pacific. Arriving at Pearl Harbor 9 August, she sortied with TF 11 on the 25th and headed for Baker Island. There she served as flagship, TG 11.2 and provided air cover during the occupation of the island and the construction of an airfield there, 1-14 September. During that time her planes downed Japanese "Emily" reconnaissance planes and, more important, furnished the fleet with photographs of them.

Completing that mission, *Princeton* rendezvoused with TF 15, conducted strikes against enemy installations on Makin and Tarawa, then headed back to Pearl Harbor. In mid-October, she sailed for Espiritu Santo where she joined TF 38 on the 20th. With that force, she sent her planes against airfields at Buka and Bonis on Bougainville (1-2 November) to diminish Japanese aerial resistance during the landings at Empress Augusta Bay.

The USS Reno (CL-96) stands by to pick up survivors of the Princeton. (US Navy Photo)

The USS Birmingham (CL-62) assisting in fighting fires aboard the Princeton. (US Navy Photo)

On the 5th and 11th her planes raided Rabaul and on the 19th, with TF 50, helped neutralize the airfield at Nauru. *Princeton* then steamed northeast, covered the garrison groups enroute to Makin and Tarawa and, after exchanging operational aircraft for damaged planes from other carriers, got underway for Pearl Harbor and the west coast.

Availability at Bremerton followed and on 3 January 1944, *Princeton* steamed west. At Pearl Harbor, she rejoined the fast carriers of TF 50, now designated TF 58. On the 19th, she sortied with TG 58.4 for strikes at Wotje and Taroa (29-31 January) to support amphibious operations against Kwajalein and Majuro. Her planes photographed the next assault target, Eniwetok, 2 February and on the 3rd returned on a more destructive assignment--the demolition of the airfield on Engebi. For 3 days the atoll was bombed and strafed. On the 7th, *Princeton* retired to Kwajalein only to return to Eniwetok on the 10th-13th and 16th-28th, when her planes softened the beaches for the invasion force, then provided air cover during the assault and ensuing fight.

From Eniwetok, *Princeton* retired to Majuro, thence to Espiritu Santo for replenishment. On 23 March, she got underway for strikes against enemy installation and shipping in the Carolines. After striking the Palaus, Woleai and Yap, the force replenished at Majuro and sortied again 13 April.

Steaming to New Guinea, the carriers provided air cover for the Hollandia operation (21-29 April), then crossed back over the International Date Line to raid Truk (29-30 April) and Ponape (1 May).

On 11 May, *Princeton* returned to Pearl Harbor, only to depart again on the 29th for Majuro. There she rejoined the fast carriers and pointed her bow toward the Marianas to support the assault on Saipan. From 11-18 June, she sent her planes against targets on Guam, Rota, Tinian, Pagan, and Saipan, then steamed west to intercept a Japanese fleet reported to be enroute from the Philippines to the Marianas. In the ensuing Battle of the Philippine Sea, *Princeton*'s planes contributed 30 kills and her guns an other three, plus one assist, to the devastating toll inflicted on Japan's naval air arm.

Returning to the Marianas, *Princeton* again struck Pagan, Rota and Guam, then replenished at Eniwetok. On 14 July, she got underway again as the fast carriers returned their squadrons to the Marianas to furnish air cover for the assault and occupation of Guam and Tinian. On 2 August, the force returned to Eniwetok, replenished, then sailed for the Philippines. Enroute, its planes raided the Palaus, then on 9-10 September, struck airfields on northern Mindanao. On the 11th, they pounded the Visayas. At mid-month the force moved back over the Pacific chessboard to support the Palau offensive, then returned to the Philippines to hit Luzon, concentrating on Clark and Nichols fields. The force then retired to Ulithi, and in early October, bombed and strafed enemy airfields, installations and shipping in the Nansei Shoto and Formosa area in preparation for the invasion of the Philippines.

On the 20th, landings were made at Dulag and San Pedro Bay, Leyte. *Princeton*, in TG 38.3, cruised off Luzon and sent her planes against airfields there to prevent Japanese land based aircraft attacks on Allied ships massed in Leyte Gulf. On the 24th however, enemy planes from Clark and Nichols fields found TG 38.3 and reciprocated. Shortly before 1000, a lone enemy dive-bomber came out of the clouds above *Princeton*. At 1500 feet the pilot released his bomb. It hit between the elevators, crashed through the flight deck and hanger, then exploded. Initial fires soon expanded as further explosions sent black smoke rolling off the flight deck and red flames along the sides from the island to the stern. Covering vessels provided rescue and fire-fighting assistance and shielded the stricken carrier from further attack. At 1524, another, much heavier explosion, possibly the bomb magazine, blew off the carrier's stern and with it the after flight deck. *Birmingham* (CL-62), alongside to fight fires, suffered heavy damage and casualties.

Efforts to save *Princeton* continued, but at 1604 the fires won. Boats were requested to take off remaining personnel and shortly after 1706, *Irwin* (DD-794) began to fire torpedoes at the burning hulk. At 1746, *Reno* (CL-96) relieved *Irwin* and at 1749 the last, and biggest, explosion occurred. Flames and debris shot up 1000-2000 feet. *Princeton*'s forward section was gone. Her after section appeared momentarily through the smoke. By 1750 she had disappeared, but 1,36 1 of her crew survived. Included in that number was

A lifeboat of survivors of the Princeton. (US Navy Photo)

Capt. John M. Hoskins, who had been prospective commanding officer of CVL-23 and lost his right foot with her, but who, despite the loss, would become the 1st commanding officer of the fifth *Princeton* (CV-37).

Losses and damage to assisting vessels were heavy: *Birmingham*—85 killed 300 wounded, a heavily damaged topside, and loss of 2 5", 2 40mm. and 2 20mm. guns; *Morrison* (DD-560)--foremast lost, portside smashed; *Irwin*--forward 5" mounts and director out, starboard side smashed; and *Reno*--one 40mm. smashed.

Princeton earned 9 battle stars during World War II.

CV/CVA/CVS-37

The fifth Princeton, CV-37, was laid down as Valley Forge at the Philadelphia Navy Yard on 14 September 1943. This ship was already in construction when CVL-23 was sunk and she was renamed as a replacement on 21 November 1944. Sponsored by Mrs. Harold Dodds, she was launched on 8 July 1945, commissioned on 18 November 1945 with Captain John M. Hoskins in command.

Following a shakedown cruise off Cuba, the Princeton operated in the Atlantic with the 8th Fleet until June 1946. She then transferred to the Pacific Fleet, arriving in San Diego on June 31st. On 3 July she carried the body of Philippine President Manuel Queson to Luzon for burial. From Manila, she joined the 7th Fleet in the Marianas, becoming the flagship of Task Force 77. During September-October 1946 she operated in Japanese and Chinese waters, then returned to the Marianas where she remained until February 1947. Maneuvers in Hawaiian waters preceded her return to San Diego until 15 March. She cruised the west coast, Hawaiian water and the western Pacific through December 1948, and was decommissioned on 20 July 1949 and joined the Pacific Reserve Fleet.

With the outbreak of the Korean War, Princeton was recommissioned on 28 August 1950, and on 5 December joined Task Force 77 off the Korean coast. She launched 248 sorties against targets in the Hagaru area to announce her arrival, and for the next six days supported marines fighting their way down the long, cold road from the Chosin Reservoir to Hungnam. Her planes then helped cover the evacuation from Hungnam through 24 August.

By 4 April 1951 Princeton's planes had rendered 54 rail and 37 highway bridges inoperable, and damaged 44 more. In May they flew against railroad bridges connecting Pyongyang with Sunchon, Sinanju, Kachon and the transpeninsula line. Next they combined close air support with raids on power sources in the Hwachon Reservoir area. For much of the summer they hit supply arteries until August, when they headed back to the States, arriving on 21 August.

On 30 April 1952, Princeton rejoined Task Force 77 in the combat zone. For 138 days her planes flew against the enemy. Small craft were sank to prevent the recapture of offshore islands; supplies, facilities and equipment were blasted behind enemy lines, air-gun strikes were made on coastal cities, the enemy's hydroelectric complex at Suiho was pounded, gun positions and supply areas were destroyed in Pyongyan, and mineral processing plants and munitions factories were destroyed at Sindok, Musan, Aoji, and Najin. The ship earned the Navy Unit Commendation and eight battle stars during the Korean War.

Reclassified CVA-37 (1 October 1952), *Princeton* returned to California 3 November for a two month respite from the western Pacific. In February 1953, she was back off the Korean coast and until the end of the conflict launched planes for close air support, "Cherokee" strikes against supply, artillery, and troop concentrations in enemy territory, and

against road traffic. She remained in the area after the truce, 27 July, and on 7 September got underway for San Diego.

In January 1954, *Princeton* was reclassified CVS-37 and, after conversion at Bremerton, took up antisubmarine/Hunter-Killer (HUK) training operations in the eastern Pacific. For the next five years she alternated HUK exercises off the west coast with similar operations in the western Pacific and, in late 1957-early 1958, in the Indian Ocean-Persian Gulf area.

LPH-5

Reclassified again, 2 March 1959, she emerged from conversion as an amphibious assault carrier, LPH-5. Capable of transporting a battalion landing team and carrying helicopters in place of planes, *Princeton*'s mission became that of vertical envelopment--the landing of Marines behind enemy beach fortifications and providing logistics and medical support as they attack from the rear to seize critical points, cut enemy supplies, sever communications, and link up with assault forces landed on the beaches.

From May until January 1960, *Princeton* trained with Marine units from Camp Pendleton, then deployed to WestPac to train in Okinawan waters. For the next three years she followed a similar schedule, gaining experience in her primary mission. Interruptions came in October 1961 when she rescued survivors of merchantmen *Pioneer*, *Muse* and *Sheik* grounded on Daito Shima and in April 1962 when she delivered Marine Corps advisors and helicopters to Soc Trang in the Mekong Delta area of the Republic of South Vietnam.

In October 1964, *Princeton* exchanged WestPac training for the real thing as she returned to Vietnam and joined the Pacific Fleet's Ready Group in operations against North Vietnamese and Viet Cong forces. Combat operations, interrupted in November for flood relief work, continued into the new year, 1965, and culminated in May off Chu Lai as she carried out her primary mission, vertical envelopment, for the first time in combat.

Returning to her homeport, Long Beach, after that operation, she transported Marine Air Group 36 to Vietnam in August, and in February 1966 got underway for another tour in the combat zone. Relieving *Okinawa* (LPH-3) as flagship for the Amphibious Ready Group, she engaged the enemy in operations "Jackstay", 26 March-6 April, to clear the Rung Sat Special Zone of Viet Cong guerrillas, and "Osage", 27 April-4 May, to protect Vietnamese in the Phu Loc area from Viet Cong "harassment."

Search and destroy missions against Viet Cong and North Vietnamese Army units followed as *Princeton* provided transportation, medical evacuation, logistics and communication support for the amphibious operation "Deckhouse I", 18-27 June, in the Song Cau district and the Song Cai river valley, then supported 1st Air Cavalry and 101st Airborne units engaged in "Nathan Hale" to the south of the "Deckhouse I" area. "Deckhouse II" and support for "Hastings" followed as Navy, Marine, and Army units again combined, this time to impede enemy infiltration from the DMZ.

After "Hastings," *Princeton* sailed for home, arriving 2 September. She deployed again to Vietnam, 30 January-19 June 1967, and again ranged along that long embattled, highly indented coast. In March, she assisted in countering an enemy threat to the Marine artillery base at Gio Ling and evacuated wounded from Con Thien mountain. In April, she participated in "Beacon Star," in the Khe Sanh area, and supported search and destroy operations in conjunction with "Shawnee." In May, her helicopters lifted Marines to the DMZ to block enemy forces withdrawing across the Ben Hai river.

A much needed overhaul followed *Princeton*'s return to the west coast and in May 1968 she again sailed west to Vietnam. There, as flagship for Amphibious Ready Group Alpha, she provided amphibious assault carrier services for operations "Fortress Attack" III and IV, "Proud Hunter," "Swift Pursuit," and "Eager Hunter." In December, she returned to the United States and in April 1969 she was designated the prime recovery ship for Apollo 10, the lunar mission which paved the way for Apollo 11 and the first landing on the moon. Completing that mission successfully, *Princeton* resumed exercises off the west coast.

After two and a half decades of service, *Princeton* was decommissioned and stricken from the Naval Vessel Register on 30 January 1970. She was sold for scrapping in May 1971.

*Information for CVL-23 from: Dictionary of American Naval Fighting Ships, Vol. V (1979), pp. 384-385.

*Information for CV-37 from: Dictionary of American Naval Fighting Ships, Vol. V (1979), pp. 385-386.

*At anchor in Havana Harbor, late 1945.
Courtesy A.L. Chaput.*

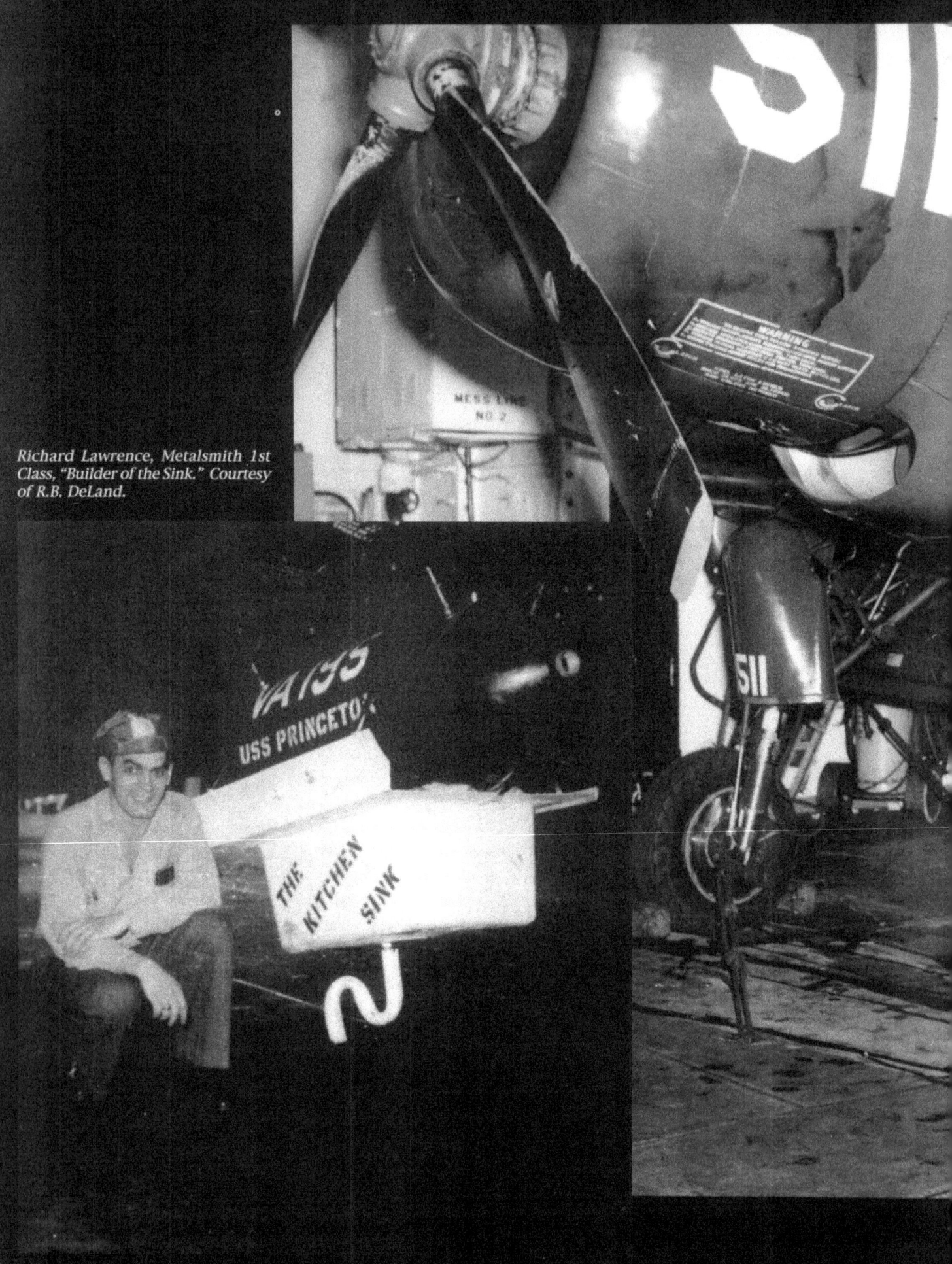

Richard Lawrence, Metalsmith 1st Class, "Builder of the Sink." Courtesy of R.B. DeLand.

STORIES FROM THE USS PRINCETON

CV/CVL-23
CV/CVA/CVS-37
LPH-5

From left: Colern, RM 1/c; Talley, RM 1; and ENS Collett. Courtesy of Richard Colern.

Our First Pacific Operation

by Seymour Parsons

The officers on the bridge for our first Pacific operation included the Flagship commander Rear Admiral Arthur W. Radford, our skipper Captain George R. Henderson and the OOD, Lt. Harry Stebbins. Our air groups were covering the occupation of Howland Island. It was Radford's first command of a carrier division. The day was cloudy with the wind less than five knots. When the time came for flight operations, Henderson asked permission to turn the ships into the wind. Radford said the wind was so light it wasn't necessary to change course. Henderson then took Stebbins aside and told him to make a slow wide turn into the wind. Using the voice tube on the starboard wing, the helm in the pilot house below received Stebbins' order and complied. Other ships followed our course. Flight operations proceeded normally with the admiral intently watching the flight deck operations. When these were completed, using the same voice procedure, the ships were slowly returned to base course. Radford then said, "You see, captain, I told you it could be done." Lt. Stebbins related this account to me and others later in the wardroom.

Question: Was Radford unaware that the ships had changed course or did he acknowledge in his own mind that the experienced Henderson knew what he was doing, that any supplemental wind would help flight operations, and that he, Radford, still had a lot to learn?

Readers may remember that after the war, Admiral Radford became a Chairman of the Joint Chiefs of Staff.

From the Deck of the *Princeton*

by Richard M. Vittetoe, Sl/c, as told to his daughter, Fay A. Vittetoe, D.V.M.

My military career began on my 18th birthday, 23 Oct 1943, when I registered for the draft at the Keokuk County Court House in Sigourney, Iowa. I requested the Army. Although the oldest son, I did not ask for deferment. By mail I was notified to report to Navy Boot Camp at Farragut, Idaho on 21 Jan 1944. After six weeks our Company 128-44 was split up and sent on a 14 day furlough. With travel time I was able to spend eight days home on the farm near Harper, Iowa. My mother, Irene, pressed a Saint Theresa holy card into my hand as I left for assignment to Shoemaker, California Naval Base. She said to always keep this card on my person, and I have. I call it my "Blessed Virgin Mary."

Time to sow oats on the furrows of rich Iowa soil, but I boarded a Navy transport to Pearl Harbor to be picked up by a PT boat, which shuttled me to the carrier USS *Princeton*. We sped to the South Pacific battleground. Day after day on the long flat top where, as deck hand, I helped to land planes on the flight deck, to park and retrieve them from hangar deck, and to ready them in the catapult with pilot on board.

June 6, 1944, I could be helping to bale fragrant timothy hay to stack in the hip-roof barn at Dad's, but World War II was in full swing aboard the *Princeton*. I was part of the US Pacific Naval Fleet in the Philippines Task Force 58, delivering crippling blows, battle after battle to the Japanese Navy. In spite of heavy losses from "The Marianas Turkey Shoot" the Japanese radio's "Tokyo Rose" blared that the U.S. had suffered defeat. As the months passed our victory counts grew as we cruised around Guam, Saipan and Tinian. The Gulf of Leyte lay dead ahead.

On my 19th birthday, October 23, 1944, while some would be in their first semester at an Ivy League college, I was on my *Princeton*, hoping to slip unnoticed to the Geedunk fountain for an ice cream sundae, there was never enough to go around. The test of my life, the big surprise was to come the following day. "Rainbow at night a sailor's delight..."

Partial clouds with rain squalls, October 24, 1944, "...rainbow in the morning a sailor's warning." 9:00 a.m. with milking chores done and the cream separated, Mom probably had Dad's striped bib overall's washed and on the clothes line. But the *Princeton* stood ready at general quarters, I near the bridge, or "island" on starboard alert for commands. Like others around me, I looked up at the drone of a "Jap Judy" diving down from the clouds. Before our gunners could respond a 550 pound armor-piercing bomb descended for the center of our aircraft carrier. Silence was all around as the bomb bored through the flight deck, the hanger deck, then exploded, along with the sounds of general quarters alarm and running feet. On deck the bomb had clipped the fueled wing of a plane, bursting it into flames. I saw Mr. Stevens of Des Moines, Iowa grab a firehose and disappear into the burning island The bomb knocked out the water pressure, an ocean around us, our hoses trickled. We were commanded to shove planes overboard before the spreading fire could reach their fuel and bombs.

From below deck smoke and heat bellowed, communications dead. The mess cooks had been up early cooking and making coffee for a day at battle, the night watch sleeping since 4:00 a.m., first to sustain heavy losses.

Our planes in the air could not find the lone Japanese attacker, who swooped low after the drop then back into the clouds as we scrambled. The *Princeton* continued to rumble as one explosion followed another. Smoke thickened as our planes landed on other carriers, our decks began to blister. The cruiser USS *Birmingham* maneuvered beside our port, racing to tether us to her. I heard a call to abandon ship, sailors jumping from all sides, five stories above the ocean. Many of those that jumped towards the portside *Birmingham* were crushed between the two bulkheads. Somehow I jumped free from the clanging metal. As I landed deep in the water and rose I felt my lifebelt slip below my hips. I was able to reach down and pull it back up to my waist. I swam away from the hulk as an explosion of the munitions blew from the hangar deck and into the faces of the *Birmingham*'s crew gathered along the rail during fire and rescue efforts. Shrapnel, live rounds, and chunks of the *Princeton* sizzled down around us, leaving the *Birmingham* with 241 dead and over four wounded as they reached to help us.

Only 20 to 30 minutes passed from the time the bomb dropped so accurately until I was in the salty water, swimming for open waters, away from the burning fuel slick spread around the *Princeton*. Trying to swim out of the path of other ships in our fleet staying to assist. I knew I was hard to see with heavy swells rolling me. I spotted a shipmate, we waved and swam towards each other, then shared a buoyant 40mm canister. There was no sunshine, but this black sailor from the officer's mess and I, the farmer's son, tried our best to stay put in 200 acres of churning Pacific. For hours we hoped Japanese pilots would miss as they flew over, strafing the water with lines of machine gun fire 13 feet apart. We tried not to see the pieces of sailors, nor the circling sharks. We'd rise on a wave to catch a glimpse of a sailor or ship only to have a breaker slam us back down.

The destroyer USS *Morrison* located us on 24 Oct 1944, 1500 hours. They tossed down rope ladders, but we were too cold and weak to climb. They pulled us onboard where we laid on her deck to warm up before we joined the other *Princeton* survivors. Twenty plus *Princeton* crew members reboarded the smoking ship as hope still existed to tow and salvage the *Princeton*. No sooner did they walk the hot deck when yet another blast consumed them all.

With salvage efforts now impossible and radar detecting Japanese planes and a submarine lurking about, the skipper of the USS *Morrison* took us to safer waters.

My father and mother, John and Irene, heard of the sinking of the *Princeton* on radio news. My mother standing at the kitchen sink, hands busy, pregnant with my baby sister Virginia, staring towards the Pacific Ocean. For the next 30 days she didn't know if I was alive or dead, but she knew I carried my holy card. It read, "I will let fall from heaven a shower of roses."

I surprised my folks with a 30 day survivor's leave, then it was back to duty in southern California. Soon after at the Chula Vista USO I met my wife-to-be, my partner in life, Ardyce Fay Wavrin. I don't know what it's like to be a millionaire; after all, who in a hundred years will know or care? But I do know I want no more in life than to smell the rich fertile soil of Iowa each spring as I plant seeds for harvest; that my wife and five daughters have smiles on their beautiful faces; and that they know I love them all.

The Sinking of the *Princeton*
by Richard M. Jackson

We were attached to Halsey's Fast Carrier Task Force in a Task Group operating to the south of the rest of the force, but well to the north of the Jeep carriers that were caught by Japanese north of Leyte. We had loaded "fish" and droppable wing fuel tanks on the TBF's during the night of the 23rd in preparation for a long range attack on the Japanese battleship force north of Leyte, and spotted these airplanes on the flight deck. Shortly after dawn of the 24th, radar picked up consecutive waves of "bogies" approaching the group apparently from Luzon. All fighters were launched and the TBFs put below on the hangar deck. The fighter pilots and those of accompanying carriers did very well in breaking up and shooting down the attacking Japanese out of sight of the group, and at about 0330 were landing on the *Princeton*. The sky was overcast at 5,000 feet. Suddenly a single Japanese fighter-bomber dove out of the overcast directly ahead of the ship. The bomb hit the *Princeton* on the port side amidships, passed through the flight deck, the wing gas tank on a TBF on the hangar deck, down two more decks and exploded in the bake shop. Several men were killed instantly. The gasoline from the TBF poured down the hole, and the resulting explosion blew back onto the hangar deck causing release of several of the droppable wing fuel tanks. The deck was awash in burning gasoline, and soon the entire hangar deck was an inferno. The torpedoes went off like giant firecrackers, and tossed the forward elevator (25 feet square) high into the air above the flight deck, from where it fell back into the pit on its side.

Ten or 15 minutes had passed since the bomb hit, and there was no change of fighting the hangar deck fire and explosions. Meanwhile the flight deck was intact, and the forward end (not directly above the hangar deck) was jammed with all topside crews and pilots. As a destroyer came along the port side, the "Abandon Ship" was given for all but the assigned fire fighting parties.

I was in the middle of the flight deck crowd and noticed several pilots lighten up for the swim by dropping their 38 caliber pistols on the deck. I saw the same pistol surreptitiously picked up, stuffed inside a shirt, pause, removed and dropped again by three different sailors, a naked display of the power of self preservation.

The sun had come out, there was a good 15-20 knot breeze kicking up a chop, the ship was almost dead in the water facing into the wind, and the destroyer (name is now forgotten) was alongside and nosed in toward the *Princeton* bow with perhaps 30 feet between the two amidships. The gun sponsons overhang on the *Princeton* prevented the destroyer from coming closer. Many men jumped or went down lines from the flight deck into the water, and swam the narrow gap to the cargo nets hanging on the destroyer's side. The eccentric wave action between the ships made this swim for some into a 30-minute nightmare of swimming the gap many times only to be thrown back just as fingers clutched for the nets. Equally disconcerting was the sight of five to 10 men slopped together in a single wave, catching the net simultaneously, and then the stronger climbing over the weaker. A number drowned in this mess, although most climbed the nets successfully with the help of the destroyer's crew. Others drifted aft of both ships and with the help of machine gun fire from the destroyer's fantail eluded sharks and were picked up by small boats.

Several hundred of us instinctively sought the *Princeton's* forecastle, which was furthest from the explosions which regularly racked the ship, nearest the water (a short jump), and nearest the destroyer (bow only 5-10 feet away). This small area was so packed with people, that as newcomers slid off the forward end of the flight deck onto the middle of the forecastle, the outsiders were almost pushed into the water. After about 30 minutes the crowd thinned out, and I suddenly remember that all my "valuables" were in the safe in my cabin only a few feet away (first one off the forecastle). The decision was made and reversed several times, but finally I dashed into the dark companionway and darker room, grabbed a flashlight stowed for such moments at the head of the bunk, opened the combination lock (1-6-9, my home street address) and tried to decide what to take. The "valuables" didn't look so valuable, and after some thought punctuated with deck shaking explosions, I tore some notes out of a notebook (number of our air groups strikes, by time and place and planes shot down) and grabbed a 32 caliber target pistol given to me by my brother-in-law as an usher's present at his wedding, which had never been fired. It seemed a great shame to have carried that pistol all around the world, never used it, and not bring it back, so I stuffed it in my belt and bolted out of the darkness back onto the relatively peaceful forecastle.

By this time badly burned members of the "black gang" had felt their way up to the forecastle, and several of us assisted in tossing them across the momentarily narrow gap to waiting hands on the destroyer's bow. This was much more difficult than it sounds, because the two bows were rising and falling at different rates causing a constantly changing vertical gap from minus to three feet to plus 10 feet. Also the bow of the destroyer at that point was only about three feet wide. While doing this I saw two strange cases: one was our communications officer in the water caught on the sharp destroyer's bow and unable to go one way or the other due to fatigue and continued water pressure. He was saved. The other was a "30 year man" warrant officer who in descending a line from the forecastle twisted it around his leg and apparently drowned in trying to extricate himself from the rope. We pulled him back aboard and left him on the forecastle.

As the destroyer's bow swung in for the final time, I jumped and landed on the very "eyes" of the bow, paused to get my balance, and instantly found myself jerked up into the air astride a line several feet off the deck. The line led from the destroyer's bow up to a flight deck gun sponson, and had tightened to a steep angle as the bows fell apart. A destroyer officer came to my rescue and then cut the line.

The *Irwin* then pulled away with some 600 *Princeton* survivors aboard. It is history how the cruiser *Birmingham* came along the portside aft of the *Princeton* to help fight the hanger deck fire, and lost or wounded half her crew (400 plus) when the *Princeton's* after magazine blew up. It is said the force of concussion was so great that the cruiser was moved 30 feet sidewise through the water, and every exposed man killed. The *Princeton's* losses were (as I remember) about 125, and the *Birmingham's* three times as many. The whole aft end of the *Princeton* was blown off down to the water in this explosion as though a large bite had been taken out of her rear.

On the *Irwin*, things were so cramped on deck that you could not physically move from the spot you were standing. At this point, the remaining fire fighters on the *Princeton*, including Captain Buracker and his relief Captain Hoskins, were taken off by an AA cruiser's boats and the Task Group Commander in the cruiser ordered the Irwin to sink the *Princeton* with torpedoes. We stopped dead in the water broadside to the *Princeton* about one mile away and fired number one. It apparently sounded because nothing happened. The depth setting was raised on number two and fired. This one was too shallow, porpoised and headed back directly for the *Irwin*. The captain rang up flank speed and hard left rudder, and the fish passed about 30 feet away on a parallel course. Whatever moral was left in the 600 survivors vanished in those few seconds. Number three was fired and hit the *Princeton's* bow about 10 feet back from the prow doing no apparent damage. Number four sounded as had number one. Number five's track unbelievably was identical to number two's and missed the *Irwin* by a closer margin.

At this critical moment, more than one survivor considered drastic action on the bridge, but then the T.G. Commander relieved the *Irwin* of the sinking assignment, and the cruiser went in for the kill. She fired two fish simultaneously, they both hit in the right spot under the forward gasoline tank, and some 100,000 gallons exploded blowing the *Princeton* to smithereens and creating the later famous mushroom cloud that rose to over 10,000 feet. A few minutes later when the wind cleared the smoke at the scene, there was only floating debris to be seen.

This incredible torpedo fiasco on the *Irwin* was not described in C.E. Forrester's article, and reminds me of the troubles experienced by our submarines in the war. I believe that our own fish came very close to killing all hands on the *Irwin*, some 1,000 men.

Later that day, as the *Irwin* headed alone for Ulithi, we were scouted out by two or three Japanese Bettys. As I recall none of the *Irwin's* 5-inch turrets were rotatable due to damage caused by being crushed under the *Princeton's* gun sponsons. The captain directed his course so that the "fixed" guns could approximately bear on the moving Betty's and the AA shells apparently scared these torpedo bombers.

The families and friends of the *Princeton's* crew who were listening to the news broadcast that night at home were jolted to hear that General MacArthur's headquarters on Leyte had announced the sinking of the U.S. Navy aircraft carrier *Princeton* with no information on survivors. Nor were they then able to get anything more specific from the Navy, until 10 days later they received in the mail the postcards the survivors mailed in Ulithi.

This is the logical end of the story, except to say that the merchant transport which took us from Ulithi to Guam to Pearl was the dirtiest ship and had the most slovenly crew that I had ever seen. The survivors were not allowed to draw swabs or brooms to clean up their own quarters, because it was the merchant seamen's responsibility and seldom carried out. We discovered also that the life boats were misrigged on the davits such that they would have fallen like stones into the water if used.

The *Princeton* had fought and survived through nine major Pacific campaigns and unquestionably had earned her niche among the nation's "fightingest" ships. She physically was not an impressive carrier compared to the CVs, and structurally was a fast floating gas and bomb storage with almost no protection. Her crew knew it, and had long anticipated her ending; but this is no way detracted from her outstanding performance in the Pacific War.

PRINCETON BEFORE LAUNCH

BY BOB J. SIEBRASSE

Several of us from the Armed Guard unit were sent to and boarded the USS *Princeton* while it was still in dry dock. Workmen were installing the finishing touches to our ship, such as welding fire hose hangers to bulkheads here and there. Electricians were stringing wire and connecting equipment in Radio One. We radiomen spent our time getting acquainted with equipment. I was amazed by the amount of electrical wire necessary. I guess they could have re-wired my home town and still have wire left over.

One Sunday morning it seemed to be extremely quiet. Upon checking around, we discovered there were no workmen there at all. We had free reign of the ship. A couple of us discovered this tall ladder that went to the bottom of the dry dock. We decided it was time to check out our underside. We worked our way down that wooden ladder and proceeded to walk around under the ship. Toward the keel we had to stoop over. I guess it was something similar to being under a dirigible. It made you feel eerie and vulnerable, when you realized the tons and tons of steel above you were supported only by the wood timbers it was setting on. Upon checking out the screws, I discovered a mass of brass larger than any I had ever seen before, or since as far as that goes. The diameter was larger than we were tall.

I assure you she was a grand old ship, even from underneath.

A/M/M 3/c A.L. Sanderhoff kneels among the planes tied down to Princeton, 1945.

SHAKEDOWN CRUISE

BY A. LEIF SANDERHOFF

I reported aboard the USS *Princeton* on Nov. 18, 1945 at the Philadelphia Navy Yard where the ship was built. My duty was as an aircraft mechanic for the Torpedo Bomber (TBM). The purpose of the shakedown cruise was to make sure everything was working properly for a new ship.

The weather was not very good, so we went into Havana Harbor, Cuba. Our intention was to have a memorial service on January 27, 1946 for the USS *Maine*, and also for some R&R. The *Princeton* was the largest ship ever to enter this harbor. We anchored directly over where the USS *Maine* was sunk. Shortly before disembarkment, a heavy storm with winds of hurricane force hit us. The ship slid at anchor and forced us aground on the starboard side. There was no tug available large enough to pull us off. Capt. Hoskens ordered us to place all aircraft on the flight deck, tail outboard and tie them down. At exactly high tide we would start the engines and rev them up at the same time. With that, the ship moved off the shore.

We departed for Norfolk Shipyard so that the hull could be inspected for damage. We were later ordered to the Pacific.

THE *PRINCETON* DANCE BAND

BY GILBERT W. VATTER

In April 1947, *Princeton* returned to San Diego after having completed its first Far East cruise. Before heading north to dry dock, short timers, the air group and the ship's band were debarked. The band was a full-fledged military style band made up of rated musicians and led by a chief musician. They had been aboard during the cruise for official occasions, public relations and to entertain the crew from time to time.

For a while, after the band's departure, a Drum and Bugle Corps was assigned to the ship. This group was made up of young seamen, fresh out of boot camp. They had been organized as a public relations unit for the Navy on the West Coast. Once they were aboard ship, they rehearsed every day on the flight deck and served as buglers, standing watch in port and at sea. They were assigned to the N-2 Division.

Late in the summer of 1947, CDR Donald F. Kelly, the ship's Catholic Chaplain, put a notice in the plan of the day. Instruments and music had been purchased and were available in the "Chaplain's Locker." Members of the crew were invited to meet with Chaplain Kelly to discuss the formation of a ship's dance band. You may remember "Straight Dope From Kelly's Pool Hall." It was issued every once in a while and contained tips from Kelly about the next port we were to visit.

Thirteen enlisted men responded to Kelly's invitation and agreed to form a dance band. The only purpose of the band was to entertain the crew at special events. No one would receive any extra pay for participating. It was only for fun and the love of the music.

The next issue of the ship's newspaper, *The Tiger Rag*, ran an article which announced, "Ship's Band Organized" and continued, "Jan Garber is worried, Stan Kenton might leave town, Dick Jurgens is sending scouts, Petrillo (President of the Musicians Union) is interested. A new orchestra is born."

The 13 men who organized the band included: Ralph Stiles, V-1 Div., Sax; H.E. Dunlap, N-2 Div., Sax; Gil Vatter, N-

The Princeton dance band practices for a big show. Courtesy of Gilbert Vatter.

1 Div., Sax; K.W. Witt, N-2 Div., Trumpet; John Lynam, K-1 Div., Trombone; Charles Hopkins, K-2 Div., Trombone; J.R. Porphy, N-2 Div., Drums; Frank Carcione, V-2 Div., Drums; R.L. Dickerson, N-2 Div., Piano; P. Mirasola, N-2 Div., Accordion; Manuel Lopez, Guitar; A.M. Fugaro, N-2 Div., Bass.

After several months of occasional rehearsals, the Princeton Dance Band made its debut on 16 Oct 1947 on the hangar deck, one-half hour before the evening movie. *Princeton* was in Puget Sound Naval Ship Yard, Bremerton, Washington for an overhaul after the 1946-1947 cruise. The program that evening included, *Solitude, Jumpin' at the Woodside, Autumn Serenade, Stardust, Stormy Weather, Johnson Rag, Flatbush Flanagan, You Do, Swanee River* and others.

Naturally, there were transfers which effected the makeup of the band. The Drum and Bugle Corps left the ship early in the game and only a few men stayed for the entire life of the band.

Occasionally it was difficult to muster enough volunteers to field a band. However, as far as I know, the band never failed to appear at a scheduled event. Usually, seven to ten men made up the group. The only time it was "supplemented" was during the Midshipmen Cruise from 26 June 1948 through 20 August 1948 when *Princeton* took an ROTC unit from Villanova College to Hawaii for training. Ten "Middies" raised the band size to 15 and helped it play four times during the cruise.

Altogether, the Princeton Dance Band (we never called it anything else) played for 21 events, not only on board ship but also at other dances for both enlisted men and officers in the Bremerton and San Diego areas. The band played for the last time on 19 Aug 1948 on the hangar deck for a ship's smoker en route from Long Beach to San Francisco.

Why did we play? Nothing was ever added to our monthly pay. Everything was done on free time and we still had to stand our watches, clean our spaces, do our jobs. The answer is, we all loved to play, our music was a lot of fun. As far as I can remember, our audiences liked our music very much. At least nobody complained. The music added something special to holidays or smokers and we were able to offer ship's dances using our own band. Not a bad deal. And, there was never a rated musician in the bunch.

I left *Princeton* at the end of September 1948 and, so far as I know, there was never again a "Princeton Dance Band" made up of volunteers from the crew.

A Memorable Cruise

by Joe Brooks

The cruise began in October 1948 and we went to Hawaii, China, Japan and Guam. We spent several weeks in port in Tsingtao, China and was there during Truman's election in 1948.

I remember the starving people when we went ashore on liberty. Hundreds of people squatted on Pagota Pier and just stared at us. We were told the Communist Army was only 40 miles away. Such poverty as I had never dreamed of even though I grew up during the "Great Depression;" all this made quite an impression on a 19-year-old kid.

We were never told why we stayed there so long. I guess it's an old Navy tradition to keep common seamen in the dark about such things. I also remember we had to keep ready to fly airplanes on flight deck at all times and if any maintenance was needed done the plane had to go to the hangar deck and a "good" airplane moved to flight deck.

We also went to General Quarters at sunrise and sunset every day. There was never any explanation given to any of us that I remember and after all these years I still wonder why?

One other memory is crystal clear in my mind. During flight operations off the California coast, I was blown off my feet and was scooting down the flight deck toward F8F Bearcat props to a certain death when one of the flight plane directors grabbed me by the coat collar and pulled me out of harm's way. I'm convinced he saved my life. I sure would love to meet that sailor if he's still alive and give him my eternal thanks.

I will say the Navy schools were great. Most of my civilian working years was as an aircraft mechanic with TWA, and it all started with the schools in Jax and Memphis in 1947.

SERVICE DURING THE KOREAN CONFLICT

BY ED BUCKMAN, VF-193, USS PRINCETON TASK FORCE 77

In the summer of 1950, I had just completed electronics school in Memphis, TN when I was ordered to Geiger Counter School in San Diego, CA. Upon arrival in San Diego, we noticed a high degree of alert and activity at the base. I soon learned of the Korean War and how it would change my life.

In a few short months, the USS *Princeton* (CV-37) was taken out of mothballs, filled with ship's company reserves and headed for the Pacific. The 19th Air Group (the only regular Navy air group on the West Coast) was assigned to that ship as part of Task Force 77. Because of the success of the South Koreans and their allies, we looked forward to a leisurely training cruise to Hawaii. Our plans were to spend ten days at Pearl Harbor. Wrong!

Two days later, we were on the high seas, planes groomed for action, flight deck crews readied, and magazines loaded with bombs. We stopped at Sasebo for fuel only, then on to Korea. On 1 Dec 1950 in Sasebo Harbor, I spent my 21st birthday with the unique pungent smell of Japan.

Our first assignment was to give the Marines at Chosin Reservoir all the close air support that they needed. Slowly they made the march from the Reservoir trap through Hagaru-ri, Koto-ri, Hamhung and finally down to the transports at Hungnam. I found out later that this was one of the greatest moments in Marine history as they fought their way through enormous odds, out numbered ten to one. Most of the Marines had frozen feet or frozen fingers. The Navy had destroyers, cruisers and battleships supplying full armament support. Then after evacuation they blew up Hungnam Harbor. The survivors of that battle are known as "The Chosin Few." At a barbecue, years later in north Texas, I met some survivors and they remembered the numbers and markings of my squadron's Corsairs. It was a thrill for me to meet with these heroes. Air Group 19 lost 51 planes and 15 pilots in close to 6,000 sorties, but we had warm bunks and no one shooting at us. The Army and the Marines took the brunt of blows from the Communist North.

Soon after, we were given ten days of rest and relaxation in Sasebo. We stopped for a beer on the base at the service center. As we left the base, we met a guy we called "Tokyo Joe," as he was always just outside the base hawking his products in broken English. We were soon to find out that you could have a huge liberty for under $2.00, anything you needed, for the prices in post-war Japan were great. After walking a few blocks to downtown Sasebo, I was to get my first insight into how different the Japanese were from Americans, a rickshaw with two very loud and very drunk Marines were yelling, "hubba hubba." They quickly told the rickshaw driver (in Japanese) to turn left at an intersection and the rickshaw smashed into a small elderly black-robed woman with a cane and San Pan hat, knocking her about three feet in the air. There were at least 150 civilians at that intersection and no one helped that little old lady. She got up, shook herself off and proceeded about her business. Human life at that time had no value to the Japanese. What a change from the protected life I had known near Philadelphia.

Our first strike catapulted our squadron commander into the water. Lt. Cdr. Clem Craig, later recalled seeing the propellers of the mighty *Sweet Pea* from under the ship. We knew they were there, but this was the first time a witness verified that they worked. Commander Craig was given a pint of whiskey to bring his temperature up after being rescued from the bitter cold water. We were never told who supplied the whiskey. Those destroyers were able to do many things that the larger ships did not allow.

Our group rapidly got the reputation for destroying bridges. We were known as the "bridge busters." Cutting the supply lines, destroying tunnels and close air support were our main functions. The crew of the mighty *Sweet Pea* won many honors for replenishment and refueling records: first jet photo unit, first group to start organized bridge-busting campaign, first carrier jet squadron to drop bombs in combat, first AD Squadron to drop torpedoes, first group to attempt tunnel-busting, first team from Organized VA[N] Squadron.

On 24 Dec 1950, I lost a friend, Ensign H.V. Scarsheim. He had broken a wire in his helmet on an air strike the day before. I was soldering his helmet when my chief petty officer informed me that we had lost "Scar" in that day's sortie. When you lose a friend, it really makes you understand how important the things you have been trained to do are and how they fit into the overall plan.

My job was to check with the pilot as soon as he landed to find out if all his electronic equipment was working well. I watched many planes crash into gun mounts and was witness to many things that can happen on the dangerous deck of a carrier. With as many as 70 planes with spinning props, deck heaving in severe weather, I still am in awe that we had as few accidents as we did. One day we had all but one plane down safely. The one plane had a 265-pound frag bomb that couldn't be released at sea. When making the approach, the pilot took a wave-off and gunned his engine at the last moment. That jarred the bomb lose. I was standing amidships and it looked like the bomb was coming down my throat. I dived for a ladder and luckily for me, I was third to reach it or I would have broken both arms. The bomb's propeller did not

Ed Buckman and Leroy Mack at a two-man tank on a square at Sasebo, 1951.

have enough rotations to alarm it and two brave ordinance men removed it from its nose-first position in the wooden deck and dropped it overboard.

Our first liberty in Yokosuka, Bob Klaus (a friend from my hometown in Norristown, PA) decided to walk from downtown and see some of the country. We came upon a small school with hundreds of children all dressed in black uniforms coming out of the school. They evidently had an English lesson that day and when I said, "hello" every one of those kids said, "hello." The hills rang with broken-English "hellos." That evening we found a dance hall and in short order we were jitterbugging with new friends to country music. They really loved the country and western music and it was hilarious to hear them try to sing the words.

Because of the years of sacrifice and war, very few homes were painted in Japan. Blankets were used to create walls. One room had a hole in the floor, as there was no indoor plumbing. Normally they had a huge pot for cooking and the women could not eat until the men finished. In Tokyo, I saw the famous police with pure white gloves directing traffic, mostly bicycles and steam engine taxis and rickshaws. The only modern advancements were their high speed trains.

In the spring of 1951, my air group was asked to burst the Hwachon Dam to help the Eighth Army. High level bombing had no effect, 2000-bombs were unsuccessful, so the next day we were able to burst the dam with AD dive bombers dropping torpedoes, bursting the dam and providing a barrier between the advancing Red Army and our Eighth Army. This story got a lot of press back home.

I remember being in a teahouse in Yokahama when President Truman fired General MacArthur and replaced him with General Ridgeway. There was mixed emotions among the Japanese about this change, about 50% were for it and about 50% against it. It took me about 30 minutes to find someone who spoke enough English that I could understand what had taken place.

Sometime later in early summer, our relief squadron arrived and we were able to return home to the USA.

WEEKEND WARRIORS
BY PAUL L. COOPER

On 22 July 1950, Navy Reserve Fighter Squadron VF-871 returned to NAS Oakland from two weeks annual training. Upon return to the Oakland Airport station, members were informed that their one weekend a month duty had been increased to full time. President Truman had ordered U.S. military support be provided to South Korea. The Oakland squadron, and 27 other Navy and Marine Air Reserve units around the country were recalled to active duty. Three days later, on 25 July 1950, the Essex class carrier USS *Princeton* (CV-37), mothballed since 1949 in a channel at Bremerton, WA, was also ordered back to active duty. Few squadron members at the time expected our term of active service to merge with that of the mostly reserve crew serving aboard

Part of Task Force 77, the USS Boxer as seen from the Princeton. Courtesy of David Gray.

the recommissioned *Princeton* on her first post reactivation combat cruise.

Neither did squadron members expect involvement in a "police action" less than a year after the squadron itself had been commissioned. Since I was not a member of VF-871, I was stunned to receive active duty orders with the fighter squadron. My routine peacetime life as a 20-year-old college student living at home was suddenly disrupted. Particularly disturbing was the fact that two high school friends, who had encouraged me to join the reserves, were neither transferred from our Photo Squadron VPP-876 nor recalled. Not only was I facing an unexpected full-time Navy life, but I was joining a new unit without the company of my two buddies.

On 2 August, after 10 days at NAS Oakland, 31 officers and 76 men were flown to NAS San Diego. A huge hangar banner greeted us, proclaiming "Welcome Weekend Warriors." The "weekend" portion was crossed out by a huge X. We began seven months of "real Navy" training preparing for aircraft carrier duty. My marriage to high school sweetheart Marie, now my wife of 50 years, was the October highlight. Intensive training included three deployments to NAAS El Centro for bombing and gunnery, two pilot deployments to the USS *Monterey* (CVL-26) at NAS Pensacola for carrier landing qualifications and two "shakedown" weeks aboard the USS *Essex* (CV-9).

The moment of truth arrived in May 1951. On 3 May four pilots, three ground officers and five enlisted men left by plane en route to the *Princeton* off Korea. On 16 May all remaining squadron members boarded the USNS *Weigel* (TAP-119) at the Broadway pier in San Diego bound for Yokosuka, Japan. There were painful personal moments for me as I watched the diminishing images of my tearful wife and mother fade as our troopship pulled away from the San Diego pier. Also aboard were members of the 9th Marine draft from Camp Pendleton as well as an El Toro Marine aviation draft. After two miserable weeks in cramped, uncomfortable quarters aboard the *Weigel*, we finally arrived in Tokyo Bay. The *Weigel* moored at a dock across from the battle hardened *Princeton* waiting for her replacement airgroup (CAG 19X). Our two reserve (VF-821, VF-871) and two regular (VA-55, VF-23) squadrons would replace the first contingent of Air Group 19. The first contingent was composed of four regular Navy squadrons. Sadly, our squadron was already reduced by one as Lt. Horace Hawkins had been shot down and was presumed killed in action. Also, our skipper LCDR William Harrison, crash landed in Korea as a result of enemy action but was rescued unhurt. The squadron had already lost two planes and one pilot despite not yet functioning as an operational unit.

Task Force 77 included the USS *Boxer* (CV-21), the USS *Bon Homme Richard* (CV-31) and the *Princeton* (CV-37), the first de-mothballed carrier manned mostly by recalled reservists. On 2 June, we joined up with the all reserve air groups operating off the two other carriers. The two reserve air groups, CAG 101 and 102, were operating with the Task Force (TF) off the *Boxer* and the *"Bonnie Dick"* respectively. CAG 102 included VF-874, another recalled reserve fighter squadron from NAS Oakland. Ten of the 12 squadrons then flying off the three TF carriers were reserves. On 3 June, a flight of

Capt. Gregg and Ens. William Hickman cut a cake in honor of Hickman's 100th landing, as well as the 31,000th pilot to land on the Princeton. Courtesy of A.L. Sanderhoff.

two Skyraiders and two Corsairs led by the skipper was praised by the commander of U.N. troops on the ground for some of the best close air support he had seen. The flight had napalmed extensive enemy entrenchments on a mountain ridge south of Kumhwa. In general, the replacement *Princeton* flyers had done well on the first full day of operational activity. The "new" CAG 19 had also knocked out two spans from a highway bridge at Pachung-jang, destroyed two rail cars, damaged an engine and two additional rail cars and damaged a breakwater at Sonpyong-ni.

The hazards of carrier air operations became quickly evident when on 5 June, an air group F9F Panther crashed and exploded while attempting to land. The explosion and aft flight deck fire cost the life of the pilot and resulted in numerous other casualties. On 12 June, an escorting destroyer, the USS *Walke*, struck a mine off Hungnam. The 26 KIA and 35 WIA was the largest single Navy combat loss of the war. On 20 June, VF-871 ENS John Moody's plane was hit and damaged, however, he bailed out safely over water near Wonson harbor and was recovered safely. On 30 June, LTJG Gordon George was forced to ditch near the harbor and was also picked up safely. Mr. George's plane was the fourth lost by the squadron in combat. On 1 July, the *Princeton* left the TF and returned to Yokosuka after 31 days at sea.

The *Princeton* pulled away from the Yokosuka Naval Base pier at 0700 on 12 July and headed back to Korea. On 17 July, squadron LTJG Donald Frazier accomplished a landmark by making the 10,000 landing aboard the *Princeton*. On the following day, squadron joy turned to sadness as Lt. Frank Martin's Corsair, hit by ground fire on a napalm run near Kumsong, failed to pullout, dove into the ground and exploded. Mr. Martin was one of the original pilots from Oakland and, as Operations Officer, was third in command of the squadron. A few days later, on 22 July, the squadron was again devastated when ENS Moody's plane was hit in the belly tank by antiaircraft fire and blew up. On 27 July, Lt. Killingsworth's Corsair was severely disabled by enemy fire and he was forced to bail out. He was soon picked out of the water by a Navy boat. His fatally wounded plane was the seventh squadron plane lost to enemy action. On 9 August, the day before scheduled detachment from the TF, all VF-871 planes returned safely but a VF-821 Corsair and pilot were lost on the final day of full operations. On the same day the *Boxer* incurred a major flight deck fire when a recovering jet crashed. VF-871's final early morning flight on 10 August returned safely around 1000 and the *"Sweet Pea"* disengaged shortly thereafter and headed for Japan. The *Princeton* was relieved by the *Essex* in port and departed Japan on 16 August and headed home. November statistics revealed that nearly 75% of Navy strikes had been flown by reservists.

The trip home from Japan included a four day stop-over in the Territory of Hawaii to pick up a number of defective aircraft and VIP passengers. Although the stop-over at Pearl Harbor delayed the arrival home, it was generally welcomed by the crew. The return to North Island on 29 August was as joyous as expected. The *Princeton* tied up at 1500 and those aboard observed approximately 3,000 wives, children, friends and well wishers waiting on the dock. The ship was greeted by the NAS band, Marine Recruit Depot band, majorettes and dignitaries. Liberty followed the brief welcoming ceremonies. The following day, an open house reception was held aboard ship during the afternoon. Later that evening all shipmates, family and guests were invited to attend a formal homecoming party at the Pacific Square Ballroom in San Diego.

Active duty for most VF-871 Oaklanders came to a sudden end not long after our 29 August return to San Diego, After the uplifting welcoming celebrations concluded, stateside Navy squadron routines resumed. Out of the blue, the Oakland enlisted reservists were suddenly released to inactive duty effective 14 September.

Officers were not affected and were to be retained on active duty for a then undetermined period. On 15 September, 25 officers and 35 enlisted men were reunited at the Oakland Airport for a civic welcome and reunion. Squadron members were greeted and photos taken near a number of battle hardened dark blue Corsairs flown north by our pilots. After 483 combat strikes against enemy forces in Korea from the deck of the mighty *Princeton*, the long weekend of VF-871 ended in Oakland, where it all unexpectedly began.

This brief growing experience left me with a conviction that the contributions of all reserve forces, ship, ground or surface, should not be left out of the historical accountings of the "forgotten war." I consider myself fortunate to have been able to serve aboard the *Princeton*, whose initial 2,500 member crew was believed to be made up of 80% reserves. Under the command of Captain William O. Gallery, the *Princeton* got ready for a shakedown cruise in record time. Only six weeks after recommissioning, she was considered ready for assignment to Fleet operations. Only 10 days after arrival with TF-77 the airgroup began flying close air support missions around the clock instead of just daylight hours. The *Princeton's* first strike on 5 December occurred three months, seven days, and twenty hours after coming out of mothballs, a Navy record. During the nine month deployment the *Princeton*, flying the flag of COMCARDIV 5, rotated with a total of five other carriers to maintain three on line. During this period she delivered one-third of the ordinance deposited by all of the six carriers operating in the area. The Princeton lead all ships in total missions flown and tonnage dropped on target. Her jets were the first to carry bomb loads into combat and her planes, loaded with more explosives than other ships, recorded fewer launch and recovery crashes. Although abruptly removed from mothballs and manned by a preponderance of reservists, the *Princeton* clearly performed her job well.

Captain Gallery suggested that the first air group contingent attack the Hwachon Dam with 12 aerial torpedoes. Although the flyers had no specialized training in dropping torpedoes, *Princeton* pilots blew out five flood gates. The second contingent was composed of four regular and reserve squadrons, transferred from other air groups. The traditional Navy five squadron air group was believed unwieldy and replacement air groups were needed. One squadron each were transferred from four separate air groups forming the new group identified initially as CAG 19X. This increased the number of available air groups and conformed with limitations imposed by Congress. The *Princeton's* second contingent was the first to test the new Air Task Group concept in combat. One unusual *Princeton* flight took place with the second contingent when visiting journalist Kate Holliday became the first woman to fly a close air support mission over Korea. Her flight consisted of napalm and rocket runs on Communist positions eight miles east of Kosong.

Regrettably, a total of 32 deaths during the long deployment were reported. Among the 31 pilots lost were two air group commanders. The many *Princeton* reservists who responded to the call during the critical first year of the war did so with skill and dedication. They proved that reserves could work efficiently alongside career Navy regulars. Their efforts and accomplishments, especially in the uncertain early months of the war, should not be forgotten.

No Wind

by David S. Gray

My two-year Navy service in Korea was quite routine except for one experience I remember where I was personally involved. I was standing watch from 4:00 a.m. to 8:00 a.m. as the engineering officer of the watch shortly after being qualified to perform that job. I noticed from the wind gauge that there was no natural wind, but that was not uncommon at 4:00 a.m. However, wind usually picked up well before flight operations launch time at 7:00 a.m. At 6:00 a.m. there was still no wind.

One boiler in one of the forward boiler rooms had required re-bricking, and was firing the saturated side only on a strict time schedule to cure the new brick cement before it could be used. The superheated steam side needed for the main engines could not be used for several more days. With only seven boilers usable, the carrier was listed as capable of only 28 knots. Several of us began to discuss what we might be able to do to get more speed. The first obvious action was to operate both electrical generators from the after four boilers, and shut down the one now running forward. The four electrical generators and the four main engines are the only users of 850 degree superheated steam. This was a change from ship's standing orders because it meant splitting the electrical load port and starboard instead of fore and aft. I ordered the other after generator started, because it tool about 30 minutes to get it ready for use. There was still no wind.

We discussed what else we could do to relieve the load on the three operational forward boilers. The saturated steam from the eighth boiler was not being fully used, so the crew began opening and closing valves to switch the needs of the galley, laundry, steam pumps, and everything else that needed saturated steam to the recovering boiler. Regulations wouldn't let us fire it harder, but they didn't say we couldn't use the saturated steam it was making. There was still no wind.

I knew my roommate, Bill McBurney, was on watch as Officer of the Deck because we had gotten up and had a cup

Mail call. Pictured include, from left: LTJG David Gray, Lt. George Wilson, Lt. Charles Tupts, LTJG Herbert Hansson, and LCDR Don Geer. Courtesy of David Gray.

of coffee together before going on watch. Soon the ship began turning in circles; Mac was searching for natural wind and there wasn't any. Still, I was surprised when a sailor handed me the intercom and announced, "It's the Officer of the Deck." The OOD almost never called the engine room. I answered, "Yes, sir, this is the Officer of the Watch," and he said, "We have a problem, there is no wind." He said without maximum speed the morning launch was in jeopardy. They were also talking about flying missions with less than full bomb loads. To a captain or an air boss, neither choice was acceptable. A carrier did not fail to accomplish its mission, or risk pilot lives with less than a full bomb load. He asked what could we do to get more than 28 knots. I told him to start ordering increased speed sooner to give the steam plant more time to respond. He said, "thank you" and the line went quiet. Normally, the bells for 22, 26, 30, or the max of 33 knots, whatever was needed to get good wind across the deck, sounded about 15 minutes before launch. It was now about 30 minutes before launch time. The bells rang for 22 knots. Suddenly I felt enormous pressure and commitment; he had actually done what I suggested. Unheard of! I ordered the third generator put on line, the electrical load to shifted to port and starboard and the forward generator dropped off line. Every order was recorded in the log. There was still no wind.

The chiefs on watch passed the word to the crew to take measures to prepare for the maximum speed that could be attained. There was really no need. Every man on watch knew the situation and what needed to be done. The bells rang for 28 knots. Soon the steam plant was whistling at near capacity, but balanced and running smoothly. I ordered the forward generator shut down. Now every ounce of steam the three boilers could produce was available for the two forward main engines. And the eighth boiler was doing its share, even if it was only to run pumps, provide hot showers and wash clothes. The ship circled, looking for wind and found only one or two knots. The bells rang for flank speed or maximum power. The throttle men pulled the after main engines open to the stops. But this was not unusual operations for four boilers. The forward throttle men opened the throttles more and pulled the steam pressure down as the boilermen fired the boilers harder to get the pressure up. The boilers were at maximum pressure. Any more would risk lifting the safety valves, a disciplinary offense. It was balance and teamwork as the crew worked to get the most out of the three boilers. Finally the *Sweet Pea* was "flying" at nearly 31 knots. It was about 6:55 a.m. A bit later the speaker blared, "stand by for flight ops" and launching planes began.

I had all but forgotten about time. It was 7:45 a.m. My relief officer was Lt. Michalek. He was a career naval officer. He was the ship's main propulsion officer, in charge of the boilers and the main engines. He was my taskmaster and the one who spent six months teaching and qualifying me for being an Officer of the Watch. He was the toughest and the best. It was his practice to take 20-30 minutes to climb up and down five decks of ladders to visit and check status in each of the four boiler rooms and the after engine room before descending into the forward or main engine room to relieve the watch.

As he approached me I knew he knew the status of every valve and every gauge in the system. He never missed a thing. He looked at me sternly. I said nothing. He observed, "No wind, huh." I said, "No sir." He asked, "Did you wake the chief engineer?" I replied, "No sir." And then his mouth turned up like the start of a smile, his head twisted a bit as if in disbelief, and in probably the highest moment of my naval career he saluted and said, "I relieve you, sir." I returned the salute and headed out to go up the ladder in a flash. I was glad and relieved to let the good lieutenant wind down the screaming steam plant.

I met Bill McBurney in the wardroom for breakfast, and he then told me the drama of how close they came to canceling or reducing the mission, but when the ship's speed rose to 30 knots and the wee bit of wind came up, they decided to go for it. All 60-80 planes were launched with full loads. The North Koreans got no day off from the air attacks that day.

Memories Of the *Princeton*

by Lowell D. Richards

My first week at sea on the *Princeton* I was terribly seasick but was assigned guard duty anyway. At night Marines assigned to guard duty would patrol the ship's interior with a loaded .45 caliber pistol strapped to our hips, looking for

Children flock to see a U.S. Marine on guard. Courtesy of L.D. Richards.

any questionable activities. Since I was so sick the sergeant let me carry and eat saltines while on guard duty, because it was the only food I could keep down. After two years of carrying a .45 strapped to my hip, one arm would swing out wide when I walked, even on liberty or on leave.

Marines also had gangplank guard duty at ports of call. I remember gangplank duty at Subic Bay in the Philippines when the sun was so hot it melted the shoe polish off my spit-shined shoes and the bill of my cap while I stood at parade rest for two hours.

During battle stations, my duty station was first loader on a quad 40mm anti-aircraft gun turret aft the Princeton's island. During live firing exercises, I crammed clips of four live shells into the breech at a frantic pace. During a live fire exercise in 1956, PFC Fred Buelow got his leg ripped open when the revolving gun platform pinned him against the lugs on the ammo hatch which had come loose during the exercise. Gun crewmembers quickly applied a tourniquet to his leg and probably saved his life.

I had brig duty for several weeks in 1956. I would teach the prisoners useful skills, like how to sing the *Marine Corps Hymn*, and I would have them practice the song during chow call on the mess deck that was above the brig.

In February 1956 the *Princeton* boarded elements of the 3rd Battalion, 9th Marine Regiment for SEATO military exercises in Thailand. The Marines covered the hangar deck with their sleeping bodies at night. The chow lines were so long they were backed up to the hangar deck. We took books and magazines along to read as the chow lines moved slowly. I was reading a paperback with a number of William Shakespeare's plays including *"Hamlet."* One of the 3rd Battalion Marines was behind me and asked to see my book. He browsed a few pages with a quizzical look and said, "This is terrible writing, do you have the sexy parts marked?"

The *Princeton* caught the edge of typhoon Sarah near Manila in the Philippines. I couldn't believe that something as big as an aircraft carrier could bounce around like a destroyer in heavy seas. Waves broke over the flight deck and damaged the catwalks along the flight deck.

In January 1956 a group of the *Princeton* Marines and I went on R&R in Karaizawa, Japan. We joined a group of doggies (soldiers on leave from Korea) for a great week of wine, women and song. I rented a motorcycle and ran all over the area. It was good times like that that helped you

Courtesy of L.D. Richards.

to forget the winter of 1956/57 when the *Princeton* was in dry dock at Bremerton, WA for an overhaul. In constant rain, the Marine work details marched from our barracks to the ship and "chipped" paint and tore asbestos insulation from the ship's pipes. During WWII my father had worked at the naval shipyard in Bremerton and I developed a greater appreciation for the work he did.

My Time Aboard the *Sweet Pea*

by Clayton B. Crosby

I went aboard the *Princeton* in October 1959 like everyone else–not knowing what lay ahead. We left for Westpac the next February (1960). Now for a guy who was from Missouri, that was quite a trip to go overseas for the first time on a ship of any kind. Now as we all know, the ocean could be so smooth then the next day it could be so rough. I enjoyed my time aboard the Sweet Pea as shipboard electrician–it was great. It was something I enjoyed doing–the good old E-Division.

It is very hard to pick out only one experience from all the good ones that I had. I enjoyed being able to go to places that I had read about in history books in school about WWII, like going to Hawaii and visiting the memorial of the USS *Arizona*–the price paid by those men should never be forgotten.

One thing that sticks out in my mind is the time we were called on to rescue 84 shipwrecked sailors on Oct. 9, 1961 and seeing the waves breaking over the flight deck–a sight to see and remember. Also, the burial at sea of two sub crew off the coast of the Philippines. My most rewarding experience was doing work at the orphanage at Dinalupihan on New Year's Day. To all the ones who served aboard the *Princeton* I am thankful I was one of your shipmates; WWII veterans, I say thank you for what you did for me and my family for the freedom that we have today; all in Korea and Vietnam, thank you all very much and God bless you all.

The *Sweet Pea*

by James Richard Cole

The summer of 1960 I was assigned to the Receiving Station at San Diego awaiting orders. Upon receiving orders to the USS *Princeton* (LPH-5), I approached some salty sailors at the base who looked like they had some experience and asked them, "What is an LPH?" None knew for sure, but thought with the first letter being an "L" it must be a landing type vessel.

Shortly afterwards 11 others and myself stood on the dock at North Island waiting for the LPH to come in after sea trials. We were very surprised to first see a carrier and second to see only Marines standing by the mooring lines.

I was assigned to B-Division's No. 1 Fire Room. After my tour of mess cooking I was assigned to A-Division's AC&R gang. My last assignment was with the Material Office.

On several long liberty weekends W.K. Lunt, David Custer, Ronald Bishop, Randall Hausler and I would hitchhike to Rosemead to the Hausler family home where we were all treated like family with plenty to eat and room to sleep.

In 1962, the *Princeton* was sent to Johnston Island where the atomic bombs were being tested. I remember the activities surrounding our participation very well. It was 825 miles from Pearl Harbor where my wife (hadn't met her yet) was living with her family (her dad is retired Navy). She and her family were able to see the glow in the sky from the tests.

The *Sweet Pea* was my home for 3-1/2 years. When I came aboard we had Marine Guards assigned to the captain and XO, brig and other positions other than engineering. When I was transferred off in February 1964 there was not a single Marine assigned to ship's company.

In the 1961-62 cruise book I am pictured testing for freon leaks inside one of the large walk-in refrigerators. My name is misspelled, but I am still proud to have been given a special place in the book.

During my time on the *Princeton* with West Pac Cruises, shipyard docking and dry dock time in Long Beach I feel that I was in almost all of the spaces and compartments on board.

My second Navy home was the *Sweet Pea's* sister ship the USS *Bennington* CVS-20. I spent three years on the *Bennington*. Both ships were in the Essex Class.

Monkey Business Aboard the "Sweet Pea"

By Gordon Boling

In the spring of 1962, the *Princeton* was concluding her West-Pac cruise in Subic Bay. I was a PFC in the Marine Guard detachment. As my dear mother had seen fit to teach me to iron and operate a sewing machine, I was charged with maintenance of the Marine uniforms in the press shop. The press shop was one of the few air-conditioned spaces available to enlisted personnel, so I slept there while we were in tropical waters.

A few Marines found that my 36-inch reach could hide a bottle in the air conditioning duct with no chance of it being discovered, so I was occasionally awakened late at night to hide a treasure. One night at about 2300 hours I heard a familiar frantic banging on my door. I opened the door to an inebriated PFC Gary Cartmell with a pint-sized monkey in his arms. It seems he walked aboard with the monkey up his pants leg clinging to his calf. He requested I keep the monkey in the press shop until the next morning, when he would get a key to an empty ammo magazine and move the little fellow into permanent quarters.

This monkey enjoys the attention on his short-lived stent aboard the Princeton. Courtesy of Gordon Boling.

All went well for about a week, when some astute Marine left a Polaroid photo of the monkey in the guard's logbook. At about 0800 hours Sgt. Martin conducted his routine inspection of the log and found the photo. His first reaction was a smile and the statement, "That's a cute monkey." He soon recognized the ammo racks in the background, at which time he levitated above his chair and screamed, "That thing is on this ship!"

Only two Marines in the guard detachment had Polaroid cameras, so you may assume the investigation into the location of the monkey was quite brief As this investigation concluded, the *Princeton* was at quarters for leaving port for her return trip to Long Beach. Cartmell was immediately summoned and given an admonishment which surely made some reference to a firing squad for Cartmell, then made a record trip to the ammo magazine and to the hangar deck with the monkey in tow, At this time the *Princeton* was getting underway and was well away from the pier. Cartmell, being of the lower 10% in judgment and the upper 10% in initiative, quite desperately liberated the monkey with his best imitation of a major league pitcher. The monkey landed in the water just short of the pier and was last seen gingerly climbing the piling, apparently none the worse for wear.

APOLLO 10
Astronaut Recovery

by Robert Carius

Apollo 10 was launched from the Kennedy Space Center on 18 May 1969 with astronauts Thomas Stafford (COL USAF), John Young (CDR USN) and Eugene Cernan (CDR USN) aboard. They orbited the moon, detached a manned lunar landing module that independently orbited, taking pictures of the eventual landing site for Apollo 11 that made the first moon landing, and then returned to the command module. Return to earth was uneventful with splashdown in the Pacific 400 miles from the island of American Samoa on 26 May 1969. *Princeton* was selected to be the prime ship for the recovery shortly after she had returned from a very successful South China Sea (Vietnam) deployment, where she was the primary afloat hospital/helicopter ship for casualties suffered in-country. Cdr. Robert Carius (retired as a rear admiral), executive officer of the *Princeton,* was selected to be the airborne coordinator (Air Boss) for the event, because he was both a fixed wing and rotary wing qualified aviator. This assignment meant that he was to control the aircraft used during the recovery and to make "on scene" decisions in case the pre-planned evolution ran into difficulty.

The lunar landing module (Snoopy) piloted by Stafford and Cernan came within nine miles of the moon's backside surface (the surface we cannot see from the earth). John Young stayed in the command module orbiting 60 miles above the moon as Snoopy was making its descent. At one time Cernan reported, "We are down among them (hills and craters), Charlie (refers to command module, Charlie Brown). Later he said, "Hey, I tell you we are low. We are close, Babe." Also, "Charlie, we just saw an earthrise and it's just got to be magnificent!" Docking back on the command module was made as planned where the three astronauts prepared for their homeward journey.

The Princeton's home port was Long Beach, CA from which she deployed for the operation. Prior to the ship's deploying, Helicopter Anti-Submarine Squadron Four (HS-4) brought most of the squadron and helos aboard for the operation. Commanding Officer was CDR Don Jones, who retired as a vice admiral. Frogmen from UDT-11 at Coronado, CA also were embarked. Numerous NASA personnel were assigned for the recovery. Team leader for NASA was Dr. Don Stullken.

A recovery helicopter from the USS Princeton hovers over the floating Apollo 10 spacecraft in the South Pacific, 26 May 1969, 400 miles east of American Samoa. Official NASA photo courtesy of Robert Carius.

Many practices for the helicopter astronaut and ship's command module recoveries were conducted near Oahu to cover all eventualities for the actual event. These practices included day and night recovery of the astronauts as well as the module itself. A dummy module that had the same characteristics as the actual one was used throughout these practices. Deployment of the frogmen and their procedures to guarantee safe recovery were paramount in these evolution's. The Princeton's ship's company got plenty of practice in recovering the module under many different conditions. This included the bridge team that had to maneuver the ship very close to the module so the ship's crane could bring the module aboard the #3 elevator. Special handling procedures were developed in case the ship's crane malfunctioned. A large mobile crane was brought aboard and placed on the flight deck just in case. NASA officials later decided to use it during the actual recovery and it worked well. Medical emergencies were practiced in sick bay and all equipment was readied for the examinations that would take place as soon as the astronauts were aboard. The medical teams assigned to the medical helo practiced their role which included the team leaping out of the helo to assist the astronauts in the module should that be required once splashdown occurred.

Accompanying *Princeton* were several other ships, including a tanker (USS *Chipola*), a destroyer (USS *Carpenter*) and a command communications ship (USS *Arlington*), but primary responsibility was assigned to *Princeton* and her commanding Officer, Executive Officer and her trained/dedicated crew.

A final practice was held near the splashdown point the day before scheduled reentry and the NASA team leader declared that the *Princeton* was ready in all respects to perform the mission. A great deal of confidence had been established during these three weeks and the crew was eager to show the world how they could handle the tough jobs in peace and in conflict.

Apollo 10's entry into earth's atmosphere was made prior to daylight, which gave Cdr. Carius and hundreds aboard

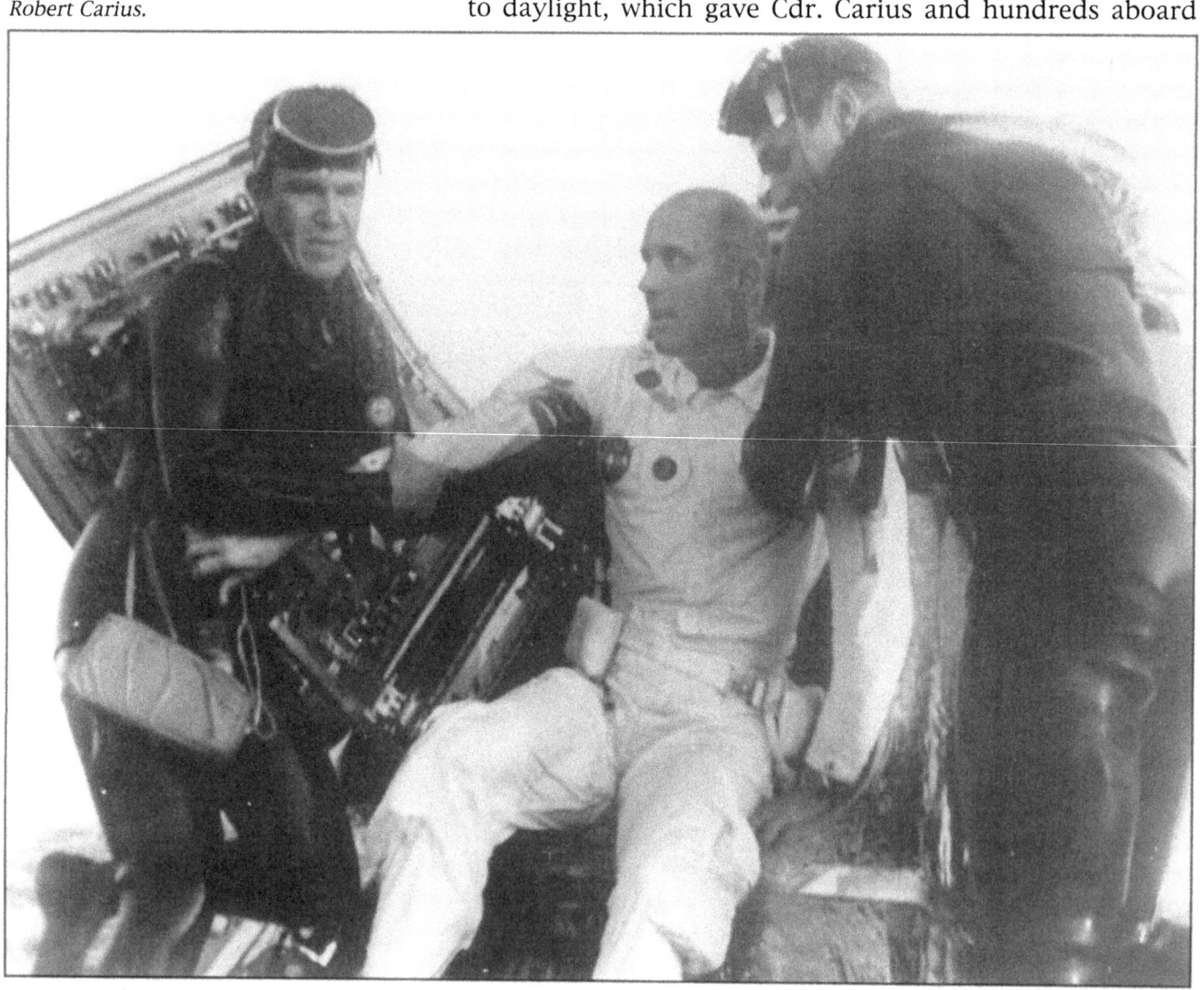

Astronaut Stafford is assisted out of the Apollo 10 spacecraft before boarding a helicopter enroute to the USS Princeton. Courtesy of Robert Carius.

ship a spectacular view of a brilliant and large "shooting star" created by the red hot module heat shield (5,000 deg. F.) that had been heated by entry into the atmosphere and the friction created from it. Re-entry started at 400,000 feet above the earth at a speed of 24,791 mph. Sky conditions were mostly clear and the sea was running low with three foot swells and a light wind (5-6 knots), a perfect day for the mission. Communications were not possible with the astronauts during this reentry time because of the ionization of the air surrounding the module caused by the intensely hot shield. Shortly after coming out of this phase of the reentry, communications were again established and all was well aboard.

As dawn was just breaking, the module's three main parachutes used to slow the descent for a "soft" landing in the water were deployed at 10,000 feet. Clearly visible to Cdr. Carius and many others, he positioned the five helicopters to their best position for recovery. Shortly thereafter, two sonic booms were heard as the spacecraft came closer at greater than the speed of sound. One helicopter (#66) that had successfully been the primary recovery helo in two previous astronaut recoveries was designated again to do that task. The special medical teams were employed in case an unfortunate situation developed and a helo for photographing the event moved closer to the command module in the

Apollo 10 astronauts celebrate a successful mission onboard the USS Princeton. Courtesy of Robert Carius.

Astronauts Cernan, Young and Stafford alongside the Apollo command module onboard the Princeton. Note the gold foil skin partially burned off the module, caused by the heat of re-entry into the Earth's atmosphere. Courtesy of Robert Carius.

waters of the Pacific. A successful "soft" landing did take place and the module remained upright which is always desired.

The news media were evident in large numbers. Radio, print and television representatives were aboard to cover all the practices and the actual event. A specially-configured WWII searchlight was modified to search out the communications satellite and to beam the signal for real-time TV coverage of the splashdown. It worked as planned. A huge NBC (the news media "pooled" their needs to one company to keep the numbers of embarked at a reasonable level) trailer was lifted aboard that contained all of the equipment needed to send the signal of the recovery to a satellite and then to stations back in Conus. Numerous messages for the print media were sent and the *Princeton* gained a lot of national and home town notoriety.

The other helos not making the pickup were carrying emergency medical personnel, and communications personnel if the reentry had occurred "over the horizon" from the ship. Air Force planes were several hundred miles up-range from splashdown in case assistance was needed in looking for the module after a distant splashdown. Splashdown occurred as programmed about three miles upwind from the *Princeton*. The "recovery" helo reached the module in record time and the frogmen deployed from the airborne helo to place a flotation collar on the module in case a leak should have occurred and sinking were possible. All went smoothly and the astronauts were flown back to *Princeton* for a flight deck welcome from the late Captain Carl Cruse and the ship's company.

The first astronaut to speak when alighting from the helo was Cernan, who reached out to Stullken and said, "Hi, Doc." He also remarked that, "The *Princeton's* recovery was way superior to any we've seen before." Once the astronauts were aboard, the other necessary events followed in close order. The ship moved quickly toward the module, approaching from the downwind side to give more control of the ship at slow speeds that were needed to come alongside the module and maneuver very close for the crane pickup. In the meantime Cdr. Carius was directing the remaining airborne helos to locate the three main parachutes, the drogue chute for the mains, and other small buoyant items. Once located, the frogmen assigned for this task jumped into the water to mark their location and the ship's whaleboat was directed to come alongside to retrieve the desired equipment. Every item that was desired to be recovered was quickly brought into the whaleboat for return to the ship.

After the short flight deck ceremony honoring the returning astronauts, they were ushered to sick bay for their after-flight physical (4-1/2 hours), and a shower. Because they did not land on the moon, they were not quarantined and had the "run of the ship," which they did take since two of them were Navy men and they wanted to show their Air Force companion what a ship is all about. Of course, NASA debriefings had to take place and occupied much of their time until noon meal. The ship's cooks under the direction of LCDR Dan McKinnon (retired as a rear admiral) had prepared a special menu for the astronauts to select their desires for breakfast. Each selected his choice and ate heartily of "real" food. Noon meal was also a special event in the *Princeton's* wardroom with the Mess President, Cdr. Carius presiding. Officers were in their best uniforms and had a delightful time listening to the astronauts speak and exchanging stories with them.

After dinner, the 250 pound cake cutting ceremony took place with hundreds of camera-toting men taking their own personal pictures of this historic event. It climaxed a highly

Astronauts Young, Stafford and Cernan with Capt. Cruse, eating cake in celebration of a successful space flight and return home. Courtesy of Robert Carius.

successful day for both the astronauts and the ship *Princeton* with her special crew of officers and men.

Congratulatory messages started to arrive on the *Princeton* within minutes after the successful recovery. From CincPac "Request that you extend my commendation to all participating members of your command for a job well done, Admiral John S. McCain Jr. USN." From the Commodore of the ship when she was off the coast of Vietnam: "1) *Princeton's* outstanding performance during Apollo 10 recovery operation noted with great pleasure, as a typical result of her customary thorough preparation and high interest which was continuously demonstrated during her last deployment. 2) Well done. 3) Captain Bishop sends." From COMPHIBPAC (Commander Amphibious Forces Pacific) "As millions saw, Apollo 10 landed on schedule in the South Pacific. Also on schedule, and in the right place was *Princeton*. To make the difficult appear routine is the mark of a true professionals. *Princeton* and recovery personnel from UDT 11 and HS-4 are so marked. You have added a new dimension to the experience, capability, and reputation of the Pacific fleet amphibious force. A most hearty "well done" to all hands. VADM J.V. Smith sends." Many other messages of similar tone were received from higher command.

Later that day (1400) the astronauts took a helo from the ship to Pango Pango, Samoa and then a fixed wing flight back to Houston (14 hours airborne). The ship then proceeded at 26 knots for Pearl Harbor where the command module was offloaded and a short visit was the order of the day. Another chapter in the active life of this carrier was closed about five days later when *Princeton* returned to Long Beach to the gleeful celebration of those families who had watched her adventures via TV as she carried out yet another successful assignment in her career. It was good to be home again. All hands were to be congratulated from the fireman in the boiler/engine room, quartermaster on the bridge, communicator in the radio shack, bos'n in the deck gang, cook with supply, handlers on the flight deck and so forth; all were key players in this one of the last meaningful missions of this great 24-year old lady of the Navy.

AMCHITKA ISLAND NUCLEAR TEST

BY ROBERT CARIUS

The next to final mission of *Princeton's* career took her to an island few people have ever heard of, located near the extreme end of Alaska's Aleutian chain, roughly 3,000 air miles from Long Beach, CA.

Amchitka Island, the site of the Atomic Energy Commission's underground nuclear test which *Princeton* supported, is one of 70 named islands in the Aleutian chain, reaching out for a thousand miles from the Alaskan Peninsula toward the Soviet Union's Kamchatka Peninsula in the Northern Pacific.

These islands are virtually treeless, supporting little vegetation. Although channels around their shores are kept free of ice by the warm waters of the Japanese Current, the weather is cold, with low-ceiling fog and heavy snows from November through April. No other area in the world is recognized as having worse weather, in general, than that which the Aleutian Islands experience. The "better" months in regard to weather conditions are May and September. The crew of the *Princeton* would soon find that the weather as predicted would be windy, cold and generally miserable; but the crew will come up to the task.

On 22 September 1969, after ten days of sailing through foul weather and rough seas, *Princeton's* crew got their first look at the barren, treeless Rat Islands of the Aleutian chain, as the ship joined Command Joint Task Group 8.3 along with the USS *Small,* USS *Strauss* and other Amchitka military units. The vegetation on Amchitka is usually described as Maritime or Oceanic Tundra. Although the tundra on Amchitka is in some ways similar to Arctic tundra, the island is more like the moorlands of the British Isles. The only trees on the island are three very underdeveloped fir trees which were planted during WWII at the old Officers Club and have grown only a couple of feet high. These trees are known as the "Amchitka National Forest."

The Atomic Energy Commission had selected the site for the underground test, called Operation Milrow, because of the island's remoteness and suitability of the area. A joint task force was established, which included all branches of the service for the operation. Marine helicopters (H-46s) from Marine Squadron HMM 163 were embarked to transfer personnel from the ship to the island. Numerous civilian personnel were aboard to monitor the tests and to make the necessary observations that are recorded during and after the nuclear blast. A large number of civilian (200) and military personnel had been placed on the island previously to prepare for the test and had to be evacuated prior to it.

The *Princeton* was the hotel for these personnel and provided the necessary support required to complete the mission. Aboard the ship was the Commander of the Joint Task Force (Joint Task Force 8), Major General de Saussure, USA, Mr. Robert Ward, Alaska's Secretary of State, Commodore G.A. Gowen, commander of the amphibious group to which the *Princeton* belonged. Captain Franklin Stephens commanded the ship and its Executive Officer was Cdr. Robert Carius. The "job" of hotel manager fell to the XO, Cdr. Carius.

Water temperatures were cold, thus necessitating that all personnel who were flying in the helos had to wear anti-exposure suits better known as "poopey suits." It was quite a sight to see these many civilian scientists struggling to get into these suits that looked like giant rubber gloves and then clumsily climbing aboard the helos. Fortunately, none of the suits were put to the test since the helos made the trips without incident.

As the evacuation from the island proceeded it was obvious that a strict head count was necessary to ensure that all personnel were accounted for. Final results were tabulated late in the day before the test and Captain Stephens, trying to pull a joke on his XO, had a messenger take a message to him stating that one person had been left on the island. The XO smelled a rat and sent the messenger back with the information that this information from the CO was already known and that the XO didn't intend to do anything about it. It ended in a standoff.

Marine helicopters also assisted Atomic Energy Commission personnel in rescuing a "snow cat" from Semisopochnoi Island, northeast of Amchitka. Helo crews lifted the 2,300 pound vehicle, and returned it to the ship, where it remained only a day before it was flown off at Kiska Island to do work on a weather station.

On 29 September, shortly after returning the "snow cat" to Amchitka, *Princeton was* forced to head northwest, to outrun a huge and strong storm moving into the area from the southeast at a fast pace. The ship raced almost 200 miles into the Bering Sea before the storm was left behind and the coast was clear to return.

The nuclear device was placed in a deep underground cavity to ensure that no fission products or other nuclear debris reached the atmosphere. Many sensors on the island and around it were to determine if that was a successful conclusion to the test.

By the first of October, the entire population of Amchitka was settled aboard *Princeton,* awaiting "zero hour," when the nuclear test device would be detonated far below the island's frozen surface. On 2 October, the *Princeton* assumed her station, seven miles off the northwestern coast of the island, some 25 miles from the site of the blast. The commander of the task force was assured that all was in readiness and the "go ahead" was given on schedule.

At 12:06 p.m. local Alaskan time, the device was detonated. Seconds later the water shock wave struck the ship. It felt as if the carrier had just run over a speed bump at a speed greater than normal. The entire ship was lifted with a sudden jolt and dropped; then no further motion was forthcoming. No sound came with the blast and no other effects were seen or felt on board. Very shortly, the scientific observers flew over the blast site to confirm that no nuclear debris had been released into the atmosphere. Soon thereafter the "all clear" was given and the embarked personnel were assembled to return to Amchitka.

A number of helo lifts later, the task as support ship for the event was nearly completed. News personnel were lifted off to the island also and most of them had a number of souvenirs that they had purchased on the ship. Press releases praised the ship, her friendly crew, good food and hospitality for such a diverse group as the news media. Higher commands also send "well dones" to *Princeton* and her crew for a difficult mission completed under tough weather conditions. As usual the crew took all of this in stride.

All that remained now was for the ship to turn south and head for Long Beach and begin her yard period which would end in her decommissioning. The ride back to home port was equally rough as the voyage to Alaska. Rough seas and heavy winter surf made the return one of the more difficult and sadly the last that *Princeton* would make as a United States Ship. Once she tied up at Long Beach on Saturday morning of 11 October 1969, she would suffer through the unglamorous task of being readied for decommissioning, but that is a story in itself.

Princeton's Decommissioning

by Robert Carius

Upon return from the Amchitka nuclear underground test in Alaskan waters, the ship's crew turned to their final task, that of readying Princeton for decommissioning. This final task may not be the most glamorous, but it proved to be most demanding and it thoroughly tested the crew's ingenuity and dedication to their ship. The attitude that prevailed was one that was a hallmark of the Princeton, and that is "if we have to do a job, let's do it the best and with as much vigor as any previous tasks." Simply stated, the crew resolved that they would smartly prepare the ship and establish themselves as a leader even in such an evolution as this. Morale remained high as plans were developed and each division received specific direction for its part in the mission.

One who has not gone through such an evolution would think that you simply packed up what you could and left the ship for the scrap dealer to handle. Not so. Very specific rules and specifications were defined for this task and personnel from the Navy's Inactivation Ship Maintenance Facility, San Diego were aboard to ensure that Princeton was properly prepared for decommissioning in three short months.

Orders began to arrive for the officers and men to their next duty station, which meant that the ship's complement was slowly declining. Key personnel in each division were designated and they would receive orders that would be executed the day of the decommissioning. Certain equipment aboard was made available to nearby ships that could put it to good use. Consequently, there was a constant stream of personnel from other ships removing such equipment, but it all had to

CDR Carius presents a Commission Pennant to Capt. Stephens.

Decommissioning of the USS Princeton. Capt. Stephens turns the ship over to the inactive ship facility, San Diego. CDR Carius is seen at right coming out of the hatch with a Commission Pennant.

be accounted for and no one was allowed to leave the ship until such accounting took place.

During an evolution like this the temptation to "remove" desirable items for one's personal use was possible. From the first day work began, the order was clear that no one was to remove items for their personal use. Accountable items such binoculars, clocks and the like were all inventoried and sent to supply locations on the base. Flammable materials were all removed, including much of the wood that was not firmly fixed to the ship. An interesting event took place concerning the fancy wood gratings that adorned the deck of the bridge. They were to be removed and personnel were vying for some of them. The XO, Cdr. Carius settled the situation by stating that the bridge personnel had first pick, and the material would be off-loaded to the pier before anyone could select their section. All were satisfied and the order not to remove any items for personal use was preserved.

The Marine ship's Cargo Officer had the assignment of inspecting, along with the XO, all spaces before they would be accepted as having met the standards for inactivation. He also had a large set of locks that could be opened with a master key, but each had their own individual key. In this manner, the division that had the space could secure their space as needed and then when it had been accepted for turnover, the lock was already in place. The system worked quite well.

All vents and voids had to be inspected and likewise turned over as they passed the inspection. A most unfortunate incident happened when a crewmember entered a void alone without proper equipment for the stale air that usually is in such a space. He passed out and then his fellow crewman also entered the void to lend assistance. He, too, passed out and before rescue teams reached them they both had expired. Even in such an evolution as the inactivation, there lurked danger on a ship of this size.

Much of the normal supply items in the storerooms had to be removed and put into the "system." That task was huge and took many man-hours to accomplish. The personnel office was quite busy with all of the orders and the necessary paperwork needed to get personnel on their way to their next duty station.

Slowly, various pieces of machinery were put out of commission in anticipation of the time when the ship would no longer depend on her own steam, electrical power and supply of air pressure. Some limited degree of preservation was accomplished on machinery, but much of it would remain aboard for sale to the salvage company, should that be the *Princeton's* fate. Most of the carriers and ships of this age were already decommissioned or were soon to be, thus some of the equipment was declared obsolete.

As communications equipment was removed or readied for deactivation, the communication watch was shifted to the Long Beach Naval Base. Food preparation was also to be phased out before decommissioning day to allow the galley equipment to be sent elsewhere. Sleeping quarters along with the "racks" were being dismantled and sent ashore, so divisions had to consolidate as more and more spaces were not habitable. All of this meant that shore facilities (a berthing and messing afloat facility) were eventually used for these necessary facilities for the crew.

Watches continued to be stood and extra watches were posted throughout the ship in case fire or flooding should occur. When most of the compartments were not occupied there would be no one there to detect these dangers. Personnel had to walk from the shore berthing facilities to the ship, as their watch was to begin. Even with this unorthodox set-up the watch standing was carried out with the usual *Princeton* attention to detail. Eventually one brow was manned with a watch team at night and the second secured.

As the countdown to 30 January 1970 approached, the ship continued to trim down the number of personnel still not in receipt of orders and the number of compartments and spaces accepted for inactivation was growing. Key crew members were still carrying out the mission of readying the ship for decommissioning, with a goal of doing it better than anyone else. In fact, there was another carrier moored close by that, too, was getting ready for decommissioning and reports from the Inactivation Ship Facility personnel stated that they wished that the other ship was as organized and dedicated as was the *Princeton* crew. That made us all feel quite good and that even this unglamorous task could give one a solid feeling of satisfaction.

Spaces continued to be turned over to the Combat Cargo officer, and the schedule was being kept without compromise to safety or inspection criteria. About the end of November all the electrical power, steam for heating and air for various purposes was being supplied from the shore. This allowed the engineers to complete the turnover of most of their spaces and to reduce the number of watchstanders. The ship was slowly going to rest after her 25 years of faithful service to the Navy. There was limited time to ponder on that because the work had to continue with the few crewmembers who were left.

As the days neared the final active duty day for the ship, plans were developed for the final ceremony. It too had to be in the style that we all were used to and had to leave one with the feeling that the good ship *Princeton* would go out with class. Invitations were sent to a number of guests who had ties to her.

Several days before the 30th, all spaces had been accepted and the remaining crew turned to in order to have a clean and fully presentable ship for the ceremonies. We all were sad that the time was upon us, but determined to put class into the ships final evolution.

The morning of decommissioning day, Friday, 30 January 1970, was clear and crisp and a perfect day for such an event. There were over 50 guests in attendance and 150 officers and men in their dress blues were assembled to say good-bye to a great and proud ship. LCDR Tom Respess, ship's chaplain, gave the invocation that started the proceedings. The ship's commanding officer, Captain Franklin Stephens, gave the final address, in it noting that *Princeton*, true to the reputation she had earned throughout the years, had been awarded the competitive E award for battle efficiency during her last years of service to her country. A few more remarks followed and then came the words from the captain that we all wished were not to be uttered; that is "haul down colors and commissioning pennant, and secure all watches." With those few words the great carrier that had served her country with distinction for 25 years through many conflicts and campaigns had her career finalized.

The ship was turned over to a representative from the Ship Maintenance Facility, San Diego, for eventual disposition (she was later sold for scrap after more material was sold or removed). Conclusion of the final ceremony was for the Executive Officer, Cdr. Carius, to present the commissioning pennant that had just been hauled down to her last captain, Captain Stephens. The crew departed with great sadness and it was a reflex reaction that as we crossed her quarterdeck for the last time we sneaked a salute to her, even though her colors had been hauled, for the last time. We also thought of the hundreds of gallant men who had served on her during all of those years and the repetition she had gained for being the best of her class.

Shipmates at attention as the Princeton's colors are lowered for the last time. Capt. Stephens, LCDR Respess, ship's Chaplain, and the ship's Chief Master at Arms salute. Courtesy of Robert Carius.

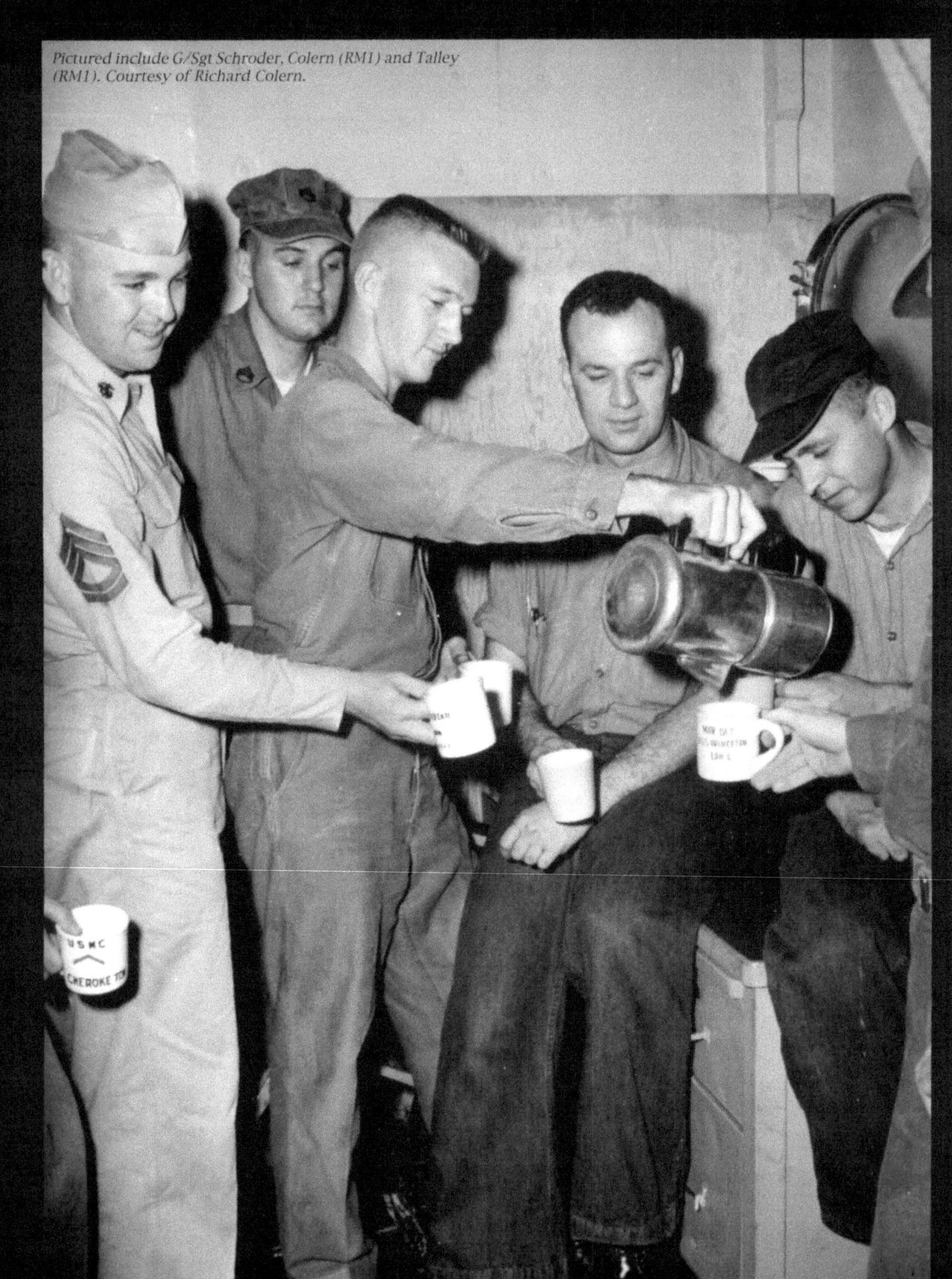

Pictured include G/Sgt Schroder, Colern (RM1) and Talley (RM1). Courtesy of Richard Colern.

Martin Herbert, Larry Keester and Gerry Neece, Hawaii, 9 Nov. 1954. Courtesy of Martin Herbert.

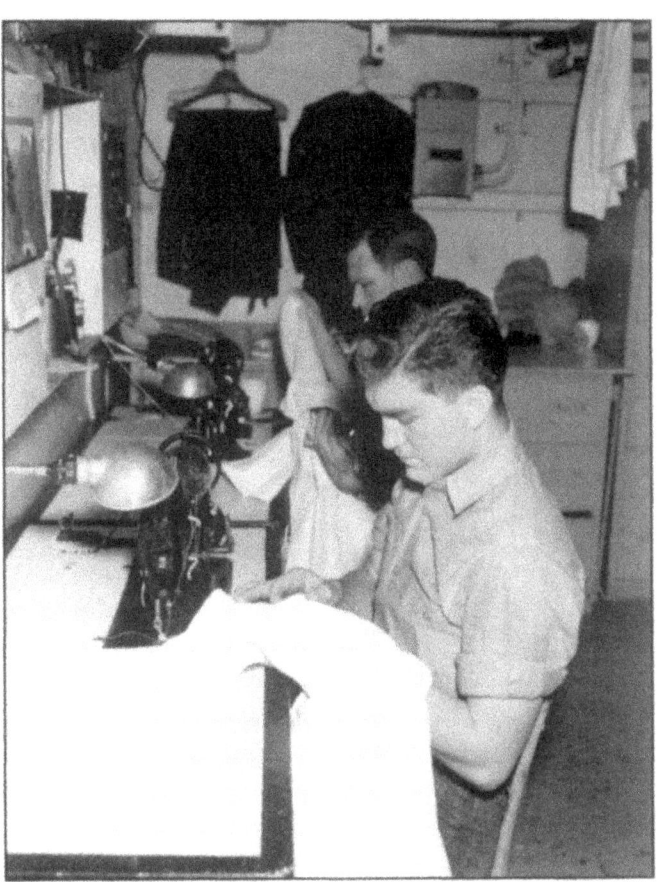

R.M. House (foreground) and E.W. McRae of S-3 Division are shown sewing markings on clothing in the tailor shop. Courtesy of E.W. McRae.

Courtesy of Norman Bell.

The mess cook's berthing area, Jack Gregg at left.

Pickin' and a singin'. R.M. House, E.W. McRae and Dallas Smith. Courtesy of E.W. McRae.

John Vitzthum, Martin Herbert and Charles Coffey, O-I Division. Courtesy of Martin Herbert.

Robert Fahan, Dick Walstrom and Carl Streble, Yokosuku, Japan, 4 July 1951. Courtesy of Robert Fahan.

The flight deck of CVS-37. Courtesy of Ronald Peers.

This group was in charge of FSK Storerooms, 1946-48. Kneeling from left: J.M. Puryear, J.R. Saggs, and J.R. Cooper. Standing from left: J.C. Creek, C.D. Chittom, W.B. Godwin, and J.W. Douglas. Courtesy of James Creek.

Princeton's soda fountain. Courtesy of E.W. McRae.

Main Communications room. Courtesy of Richard Colern.

Bottom row: Sanders, Grisamore, Cavanaugh, Huber, Bolton, Leichy, Tom, Shenkenburger, and Mullen. Back row: Brachmonte, Seipel, Colern, and Wright. Courtesy of Richard Colern.

Captain F. Massie Hughes, first commanding officer of the USS Princeton, 19 June 1947. Courtesy James Creek.

The Tiger Balm Garden, Hong Kong, 13 March 1955. Courtesy of Martin Herbert.

David Bruny, Gerry Neece and Martin Herbert, Hawaii, 9 Nov. 1954. Courtesy of Martin Herbert.

Robert Fahan, 1950.

Courtesy of K.S. Rapp.

Courtesy of Richard Colern.

Martin Herbert and younger brother Leo Herbert, both in O-I Division.

One of Princeton's AF-4Us up close. Courtesy of Jerry Nemerovsky.

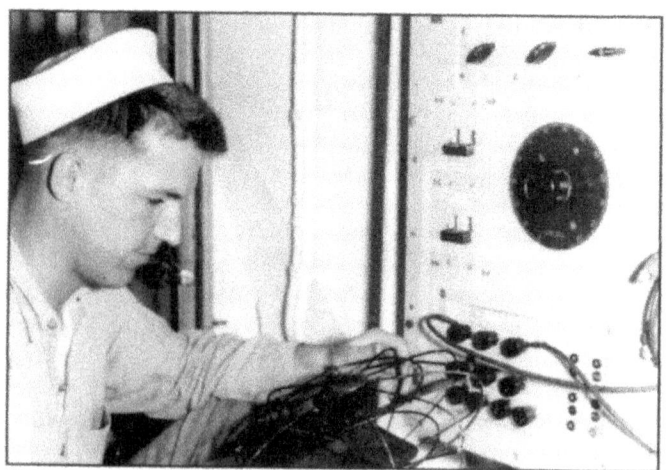
George Kolar in the after lighting shop.

Jerry Nemerovsky takes a rick-a-shaw ride in Japan, June 1952.

Dick Brookhart and Graham Brest, Korea, May 1952.

Robert Fahan on the flight deck.

George Kolar on left.

Gail Keith on top of a twin 5"/38 gun mount on the Princeton.

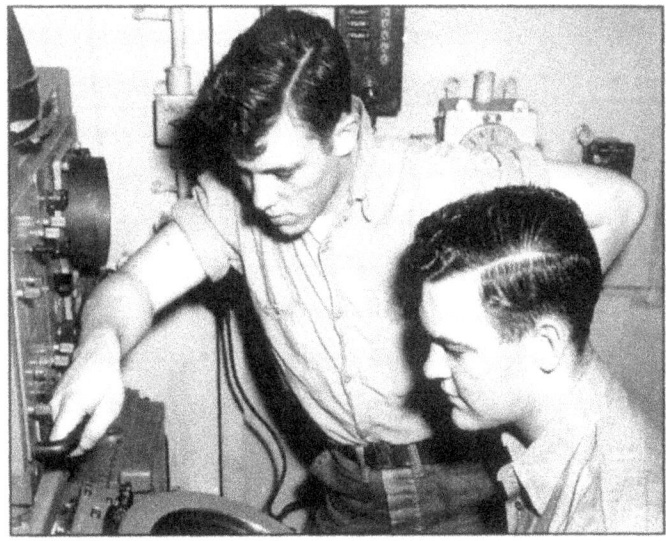
Martin Herbert and Leo Herbert, 1954.

Jack Ogilvie, Raymond Gary, and Harold Bollinger, July 1951. Courtesy of Graham Brest.

USS Princeton (LPH-5) refueling from USS Chipola (AD-63) during operations in the Pacific, 25 June 1968. (Official U.S. Navy photograph by Photographer's Mate 3rd Class Carty, USN 1142529)

USS Princeton (LPH-5) on her "Last Voyage," Portland, Oregon, 1970.

The USS Princeton (CV-37/LPH-5) Reunion Group History

The group's first reunion was held at the commissioning of the new USS *Princeton* (CG-59), a guided missile cruiser, at the shipyards in Pascagoula, MS, in 1989. Thirty-five shipmates and their wives attended. In 1992, over 450 shipmates and their wives and friends attended the second reunion in San Diego. Many shipmates were reunited, some after more than 40 years. A great time was had by all. The vote at that reunion was to hold the next one in 1994 at Charleston, SC. Again, over 450 attended. Many excellent tours were enjoyed, and to top it all off, the reunion banquet was held on the hanger deck of the USS *Yorktown*, a museum ship anchored in Charleston harbor. At this business meeting the vote was to hold the next reunion in Las Vegas, in 1996.

Everyone thoroughly enjoyed the meeting in Las Vegas. The vote here was to have the next meting in Pensacola Beach,

FL in 1998. Everyone enjoyed the great hospitality of the Hampton Inn. The banquet was held at the Naval Air Museum; the history of Naval Air is all there.

Over 400 shipmates and wives attended the 2000 meeting in Seattle, WA, over the 4th of July. It was a great city with many great tours.

In April 2002 the group met in Corpus Christi, TX, with the banquet held on the hanger deck of the USS *Lexington*. The group will meet again in 2004 at Norfolk, VA, home of the largest naval bases in the United States.

The group has grown to include a roster of 4,800 shipmates. Almost 600 of these are dues-paying members. A USS *Princeton* website has been developed, and an 11-man board of directors is always busy seeing that the organization stays strong and that all enjoy the reunions.

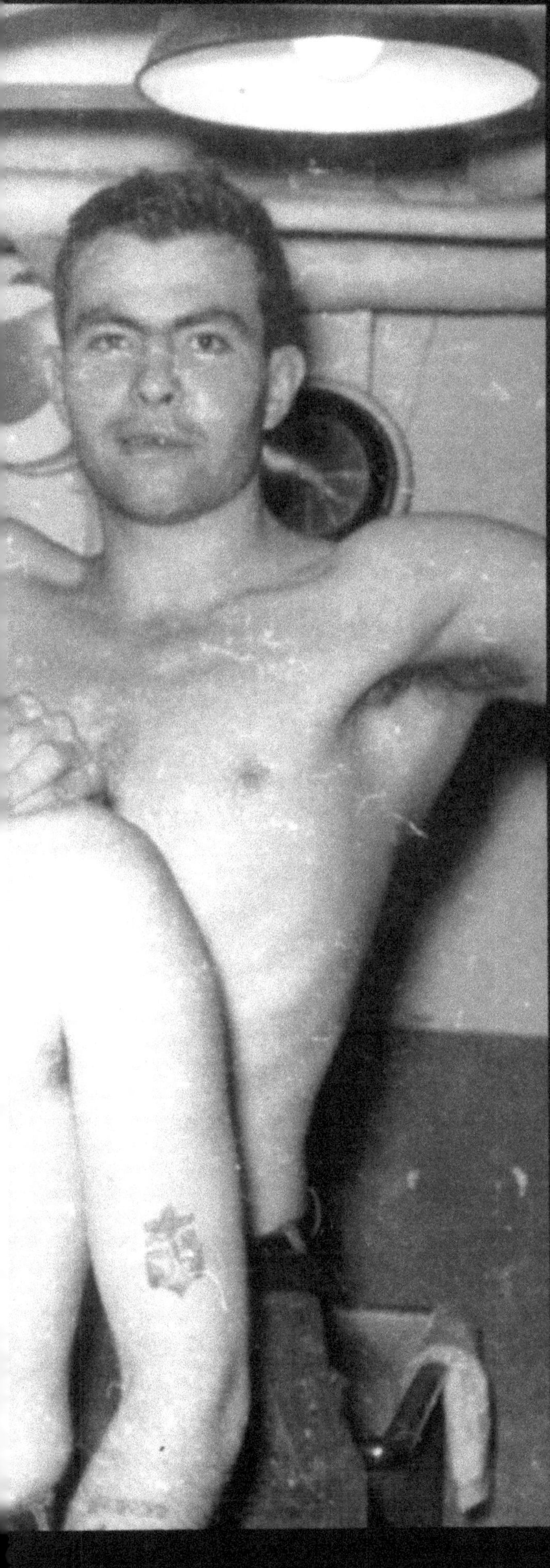

BIOGRAPHIES
OF THE

USS
PRINCETON

CV/CVL-23
CV/CVA/CVS-37
LPH-5

Harold Gamblin, C.F. Sandifer, R.E. Kagy, and J.C. Shoup in the laundry room, 1952. (Courtesy of R.E. Kagy)

DONALD LEE ALDER, born Sept. 9, 1942 in Longview, WA. Graduated from Kelso High School in 1961 and attended Lower Columbia College. Joined the USN Jan. 15, 1964 in Flagstaff, AZ. Stationed at Subic Bay, P.I., he worked in Combat Cargo (USMC Division).

Participated in Da Nang Relief Operation, November 1964; Operation Jackstay, April 1965; Operation Hastings July-August 1966; Operation Hickory and Operation Beau Charger, May 1967. He spent 35 months overseas. In April 1967 he was voted USS *Princeton* Man of the Month. Discharged Dec. 16, 1967 with rank of SNE3.

Worked 23 years at Sears as an auto mechanic and is now employed with Safeway. Married to Katherine M. Tidmarsh for over 35 years and has two daughters, Tamra Waldo and Trece Warren; four grandchildren: Travis, Ashley, Rachel and Abigail.

NORMAN HENRY BELL, born in Perry, GA. Joined the USN in 1934 and received boot training at Newport News, VA. His sea service began and ended in the Pacific area. Served aboard the USS *Langley*, USS *Zane (nine years)*, USS *Boxer*, USS *Marcus Island*, USS *Princeton*, USS *Calvert*, VP-48 and VP-50. As a Pearl Harbor survivor aboard the USS *Zane* on Dec. 7, 1941, he was cited by Adm. W.F. Halsey for skillful and effective performance of duty.

Shipmate Bell also received Letters of Commendations from James B. Kisner, CO, Fighter Squadron 791; W.A. Sullivan, CO, NAS Kingsville, TX; and COM Treasurer J.B. Brown at NAS Whidbey Island, WA; W.E. Premo Jr., CO NAS Iwakuni, Japan; S.J. Michael, CO, NAS Alameda, CA; and H.E. King, Acting Air Base Commander, Marine Aircraft Group 12, Iwakuni, Japan, 1st Marine Aircraft Wing. He was also featured in the *SEA HAWK*, the Fleet newspaper and in the national *JET* magazine for his work with the Aijino-ie Orphanage.

Awarded Good Conduct Medal, APCM w/4 stars, China Service, Korean Service, Philippine Liberation w/4 stars, American Theater, UN Medal, Navy Unit Citation, WWII VM and Pearl Harbor Survivor Medal.

After Chief Bell's retirement from the USN, he graduated from Laney College and displayed the same zeal and dedication in his involvement with veterans organizations and community activities. His pride in the Navy and his loving concern for the shipmates with whom he had served during WWII and the Korean Conflict have never diminished. Bell and his wife Mae have one son and two grandchildren.

JAMES M. BENDER, born July 22, 1932 in Walnut Ridge, AR. Graduated from Leuzinger High, Lawndale, CA in 1950. Joined the USN in September 1950 and served on the USS *Princeton* (CV-37). His greatest experience has to be his time served in the *Princeton* and the people he served with.

Discharged June 1954 as BT3/c. Awards include the National Defense Service Medal, UN Service Medal, Korean Service Medal w/6 stars and Navy Occupation Medal (Asia).

Retired as president, IBT Local 224, Los Angeles, CA in June 1990. Married to Patricia for over 47 years, he has four children: Alan, Karen, Susan and Daniel; five grandchildren and three great-grandchildren.

He is looking forward to the next reunion.

RAY BURTON BOLEY, born June 9, 1925 in Hominey Falls, WV. Enlisted in USMC Oct. 23, 1942 and received basic training at Parris Island, SC. Also spent two weeks on the rifle range and six weeks in Sea School in Norfolk, VA at Portsmouth Navy Yard. From there he boarded the USS *Princeton* and traveled from the Atlantic to the Pacific Ocean. He remained on the ship until it sank Oct. 24, 1944 and spent two hours and 45 minutes in the water with only a life jacket until he was picked up by a destroyer.

He transferred to a troop ship, came into Pearl Harbor; rested a few days, re-outfitted and was sent to Camp Pendleton, CA. He was given a 30-day leave and travel time to get to Washington, DC where he spent four months duty guarding Belleville, MD, Research Center. Spent six weeks in Camp Lejeune, NC training in land-infantry and was sent back to Camp Pendleton as part of the 6th Marine Division, preparing to go overseas. Japan surrendered and he did not have to go. Spent the rest of his time in commissary duties in San Diego.

Discharged Sept. 25, 1945, he received a commendation Nov. 11, 1944 for Meritorious Conduct displayed while serving on the *Princeton* from June 11, 1944 to the sinking of the ship. At the time of the sinking, the ship was engaged in offensive operation against the enemy off the east coast of Luzon, PI. He also received special recognition as a light anti-aircraft gun crewman and at least five engagement stars during his service.

After discharge he went to work in the mines for Nicholas-Webster Coal Corp. on Oct. 18, 1945. After three years he transferred to Mount Hope Coal Co. at Holcomb, WV, which later became Pitson Coal of Huntington. He retired Dec. 31, 1986.

Married Euvenia Mullens Dec. 24, 1945 and has three daughters, eight grandchildren and six great-grandchildren.

DURLEY K. "KEN" BOYER, born Sept. 17, 1929 in Belle Fourche, SD. Joined the service June 27, 1951 and was stationed at Yokuska and was in Korean waters 1954 until his discharge in June 1955 as YN3.

Retired September 1992 from South Dakota Service. He is a life member of the VFW and the American Legion. Presently he serves as the adjutant for Lamnison Post 147 and is the County Veteran Service Officer.

Married to Nora, he has three children: Guyla, Douglas and Bryan and one granddaughter, Stephane Powers.

WILLIAM LEE BRATCHER SR., born June 25, 1926 in Manchester, MD. Graduated from high school plus USN and American Banking equal two years college. Joined the service in 1944 and served on the USS *Princeton*. Discharged in 1946 as AOM2/c.

He retired in January 1985 as a senior banking officer.

Married to Myrle Eileen and has two children, William Jr. and Eric, and four grandchildren.

GRAHAM K. BREST, born July 8, 1932 in New Castle, PA. Attended two years of college. Enlisted in the USN Aug. 7, 1950 and served in Korea, 1950-54.

He has a number of memories with four months of duty in B Division, Fireroom No. 1 and 39 months in E Division. However, his most memorable experience was meeting his younger brother at sea in 1952. He was serving on the USS *Cimarron* AO-22 as a fireman apprentice. On June 26 and July 14, 1952 while refueling, he was granted permission to talk to his brother via the sound powered phone. They could see each other, but were separated by several hundred feet of the Sea of Japan. He had not seen his brother since August 1950. Although talking and seeing him from a distance was very satisfying, he decided he wanted to visit him. It was approved July 31, 1952 and he had the privilege and excitement of riding the high line to the USS *Cimarron*. They had an enjoyable visit which turned out to be the last time until they were both discharged in mid-1955.

The second thrilling experience was flying from the carrier. For many airdales, this is no big thing, but for a ship's company enlisted man, it was a real thrill. After transferring to E Division, he was approved for Electrician Mate School in San Diego, CA. The *Princeton* did not return to the US as scheduled in May 1951. Air Group 19X relieved Air Group 19. His orders could not be changed so he flew from the fleet to the US to enroll in school Aug. 2, 1951. Discharged May 27, 1954 as PO3/c.

Retired in May 1995 after 26 years as an US Army civilian. Married Marian on Dec. 16, 1952 and has three children: Lisa Miller, Randall and Brian; seven grandchildren: Lindsay, Megan and Justin Brest; Brittney and Caitlin Gallion; and Tyler and Austin Brest.

CHARLES K. BRIGHTON, born March 31, 1935 in Bellingham, WA. Enlisted in the USN at age 16 and left on April 4, 1952. Boot camp was in San Diego for 11 weeks. His orders read Whidbey Island, WA (Ault Field) for a P2V School, but he was sent to the Far East for further assignment.

Left San Francisco aboard the USNS *Gen. D.I. Sultan*, taking 17 days to get to Guam. Volunteered for the NAS Agana Security Dept. and was there for 18 months (for 17 days of that time he was part of the security for the President of the U.S. and the President of the Philippines). Left Guam for HU-1 San Diego then to the USS *Princeton* (CVS-37). He was part of the V2 Division Port Barrier crew and ship's company from October 1954 to February 1956.

In November 1952 he started writing a buddy's sister (Doris) in Washington state and married her in June 1954 (yes, she's still my girl). He and Doris were aboard the *Princeton* for the Wives Cruise Dec. 2, 1955 and had their picture taken with Capt. and Mrs. H.G. Sanchez, CO. Doris received a certificate as Honorary Sub Sinker and he received a certificate promoting him to AB-3. He left the USN in February 1956 and returned April 1, 1958 to Attack Squadron 65 aboard the USS *Midway* (CVA-41). Discharged for the second time in October 1959. Awards include the China Service, National Defense, United Nations and Korean Service.

Retired Aug. 1, 1998 after 30 years with the city of Kelso in traffic control. He has three daughters, nine grandchildren and eight great-grandchildren.

JOE C. BROOKS JR., born Jan. 4, 1929 in Broken Arrow, OK. Joined the USN Oct. 1, 1946 and served on the USS *Princeton* (CV-37) during 1947-48. In 1948 he made the trip to Tsingtao, China, Japan and Guam. Discharged Oct. 11, 1949 as AMM3/c.

He retired Sept. 1, 1985 as a mechanic from Trans-World Airlines. Joe and his wife Mary Jo have three children: Michael Ray, Vickie Maurine and Mark Wayne; four grandchildren: Alexander, Sterling, Jonathan and Amy.

ROBERT BUTLER, born March 12, 1929 in Williams, IA. Joined the USN in May 1948 and spent two years at the Fleet Aviation Accounting Office at North Island, San Diego. Boarded the *Princeton* at North Island in 1950 and served in her until 1952 in aviation supply. Discharged May 22, 1952 and received one Battle Star.

He retired in March 1989 from Case-International Co. His most enjoyable times were aboard the *Princeton*. It was a great experience during the Korean War to take part in the operation of that great ship. He is still in contact with the many good friends that he served with. He has been involved in helping put together reunions of the *Princeton* since 1990. It has been a rewarding experience helping to get shipmates together again after so many years.

Robert and his wife Gloria have four children: Dennis, Debra, Darcia and Angie; and three grandchildren: Melissa, Collin and Erin.

ED BUCKMAN, born Dec. 1, 1929 in Norristown, PA. Attended one year of college and joined the USN Oct. 11, 1948, Sea of Japan/Chosin Reservoir, November 1950-May 1951.

Memorable Experiences: went through the coldest winter he ever experienced with snow on the flight deck; also, one night while doing figure eight maneuvers, they lost a jet plane when the cable broke and it went over the side. Discharged Oct. 10, 1952 as AT3 electronics technician.

Retired in January 1992 and does volunteer work, part-time fun jobs and US Post Office during the holidays. Resides in Hurst, TX.

Married to Jody for over 42 years, he has four children: Marlene, Debbie, Mike and Patti; eight grandchildren: Amie, Andy, Matt, Kate, Micheal, Chris, Nick, Kristin and one great-grandchild, Ryan.

RUSSELL H. CANNON, born Sept. 9, 1944 in Fairfax, OK (Osage Indian Reservation). He has an AS and BS degrees in mechanical technology. Joined the US Army (NG) in 1961, 45th Inf. Div., Charley Co. This was the only all Indian company in the Army and was located at Chilocco Indian School, OK.

Transferred to the USN in January 1962 and after boot camp stationed aboard the USS *Princeton* (LPH-5) until discharged. He then rejoined the 45th Div., Charley Co. until the famed all Indian company was ordered disbanded due to the perception of segregation. SSgt. Cannon was the last Indian discharged from the company.

Served on the USS *Princeton* and participated in the evacuation and protection of officials from the islands of Que Moy and Mat Su in the Formosa Straits, 1962; the atomic testing that took place at Johnson Island and the amphibious landing at Da Nang and Chu Lai Beach in 1965. While waiting for the processing of discharge at the Long Beach Navy Station he was assigned to riot control duty in Watts.

He recalls the atomic test, the friends made and the trust in one another, the amphibious landings, the different cultures of the native people and the opportunity to participate in some of them and liberty in Olongapo, PI. Discharged from the Navy in Aug. 17, 1965 as BT-2 and from the Army in 1972 as staff sergeant.

Retired from the US Bureau of Indian Affairs Dec. 31, 1999. He has three children: Justin, Teresa and Alyssa.

ROBERT CARIUS, born Jan. 4, 1929 in Peoria, IL. Attended US Naval Academy (1951-BS), Naval Postgraduate School (1958-BS) and Iowa State College (1959-MS). Joined the USN July 9, 1947 and participated in various South China Sea (Vietnam) deployments, 1956-73.

Included among his memorable experiences: being airborne coordinator for Apollo 10 astronaut recovery, 1969; executive officer of *Princeton* during Amchitka Island nuclear tests and at time of ship decommissioning; CO of USS *New Orleans* (Vietnam deployments and astronaut recovery for Skylab 2); CO of flagship for demining of Haiphong Harbor during peace talks; two tours in Pentagon (R&D for one and head of aviation programs for second); aviation squadron command and air group command; shore duty tour at Atomic Energy Commission and both fixed wing and rotary-wing aviation qualified.

Retired as rear admiral Sept. 1, 1981. He was employed as a professor of physics and mathematics at Arkansas College and still works as a builder of homes.

Married to Geraldine "Gerry," he has six children: Patricia, Mary, Linda, Robert, Daniel and Sara; eight grandchildren: Kristin, Kathleen, Christopher, Matthew, Mary Beth, Kyle, Nicole and Ashly.

ARTHUR L. CHAPUT, born June 22, 1925 in Pawtucket, RI. Enlisted in the USN Oct. 1, 1942, age 17. He completed many technical schools and the remainder of his tour of duty was served on the East Coast. He remembers loading planes with depth charges to destroy German U boats sighted off the coast of Rhode Island.

He was never called for overseas service except for a short term on the USS *Princeton*. In late 1945 they boarded her for a shakedown cruise to Havana, Cuba. After that tour of duty and because they were no longer at war, he was eligible for discharge March 21, 1946 as AOM1/c. Some call it luck, but he knows that to be in the service during war time and never have to leave the shores of the US is a gift that was allotted to very few. He thanks God for His protection then and even to this day.

Retired in 1987 after self-employed at Day N' Nite Appliance Service.

Married to Rollande Y. Robichaud and has five children, 14 grandchildren and two great-grandchildren.

THOMAS "TOM" COBB, born May 8, 1944 in Memphis, TN and graduated from Arkansas State University. He joined the USNR in 1966 and served on the USS *Princeton* (LPH-5), Vietnam. Discharged in 1972 as FTG2.

He will retired June 2002 as an investigator for State Farm Insurance. Married to Jan and has a daughter Denise, stepson Mark and grandchildren, Zack, Jordan and another on the way.

ORVILLE E. "LOU" COCKLEY, born Nov. 15, 1927 in St. Louis, MO and is a graduate of UCLA, Class of 1951 in business administration. Joined the USN March 13, 1946.

He was an electronic technician's mate and had the first duty in Communication/Transmitter Room when USS *Princeton* went on a shakedown cruise after dry-dock in Bremerton, WA in 1947. Captain called down from the bridge, yelling that the transmitter wasn't working and he couldn't communicate with anyone. He was really upset! This was Cockley's first serious duty/responsibility and he was very nervous. Luckily he found a switch in the wrong position and flipped it and the transmitter worked. That was the highpoint of his "Battle/Campaigns." Discharged Jan. 14, 1948 as ETM3/c.

He retired in May 1999 as a vending business owner. Married to Mary Susan, he has three children: Wendy, Julie and Lori.

JAMES R. COLE, born July 2, 1941 in Hammond, IN. Graduated from Antioch Township High School. He joined the USN Feb. 23, 1960 and participated in four WESTPAC cruises, Vietnam. Discharged Sept. 28, 1967.

He has been employed with Abbott Laboratories since Jan. 23, 1978. Married to Margaret and has one son Edward.

RICHARD M. COLERN, born July 21, 1928 in Buffalo, NY. He joined the USN Jan. 11, 1946. Assignments included COMNAVPHIL., USS *Sperry*, *Gen. Randall*, MSTS Seattle, WA; MSTO Portland, OR and USS *Princeton* (LPH-5).

Among his memorable experiences were Operation Dominic (A-Bomb test); the *Princeton* being flag ship for JTF-8 at Johnson Island; witnessing

12 atomic devices detonated; the *Princeton* delivering Army MAG units, OB aircraft and helicopters to Vietnam in 1963; rendezvousing with the USS *Wasp* to pick up President Eisenhower's helicopters to be delivered to Japan for upcoming visit (which was canceled due to demonstrations in Japan); lifeboat duty in the USS *Sperry* (AS-12), 1948; rendezvousing with USS *Ronquil* off San Diego to take a sick shipmate off for medical treatment. He retired in May 1965 at Point Magu.

Employed as a correctional officer for the state of California, Chino, CA, he retired after 24 years in 1987.

He married Pauline M. Peternell from San Diego, CA and has four children: Michael, Shane, Kathy and Denise, and two granddaughters, Leslie and Diana.

PAUL L. COOPER, See Special Story

JAMES C. CREEK, born June 17, 1924 in Evansville, IN. He joined the USN Oct. 13, 1942. Served in USS *Princeton* (CV-37) from June 1946 to September 1948. He recalls the week they took aboard jet aircraft and all crash landed since the landing gear was not strong enough for carrier landings. He retired as lieutenant SC April 1, 1967.

Retired from International Multifoods, sales and technical service in July 1983. Married to Marilyn and has seven children, 18 grandchildren and five great-grandchildren. He is legally blind.

CLAYTON B. CROSBY, born Sept. 4, 1932. He graduated from Eugene Bible College in pastoral studies. Joined the USN on March 16, 1959 and served in the South Pacific. Discharged Feb. 7, 1963 as E-5.

He retired Sept. 5, 1997. Married to Mary Belle (passed away Jan. 9, 1998) and has four sons: Dennis, Ray (20 years in the Army), Gary Dale, Clayton Eugene, and 10 grandchildren.

GARY DAY, born March 18, 1947 in Sparta, TN. Graduated with a BS in business management from Tennessee Tech in 1973. He joined the USN on April 26, 1966 and served three Vietnam tours aboard the *Princeton* (1966-68) and one tour to pickup Apollo-10 in the South Pacific in 1969. Discharged Nov. 3, 1969 as AK3 E-4.

He is employed in transportation operations, Federal-Mogul in Tullahoma, TN. Married over 34 years to Darnell, he has two children, Will and Wendy, and a granddaughter, Taylor Cowley.

ROYAL BERKLEY DELAND, born May 4, 1919 in Magna, UT. He graduated from high school and joined the USN September 1940. Assignments included Saipan, USS *Princeton*, Japan and USS *Lake Champlain*. Retired in June 1961 as CWO2.

Employed as director of Roque River Senior Club, he retired in June 1995. Married to Neoma and has three children: Donald, Royal and Darilyn; and seven grandchildren: Tammi, Jamie, Richard, Tracy, G.G., Amanda and Josh.

PHILLIP W. DEPAUK JR., born Sept. 22, 1946. Received a BSEE and MS in systems management. He joined the USN Aug. 4, 1966 and served in the USS *Princeton* (LPH-5), Vietnam 1968.

He recalls WESTPAC (Vietnam) tour in 1968, Apollo-10 recovery in 1969, Singapore, Japan and Atomic Energy Commission test Event Milrow, October 1969, Amchitka Island, AK. Discharged Sept. 22, 1972 as ET1.

He is employed as project manager with Space and Naval Warfare Systems Command.

Married to Kathryn Brooke and has two children, April Dawn and Eric Phillip.

MARION FRANKLIN "FRANK" DEPAUK, born April 26, 1950 in Van Nuys, CA. Received an AA in business administration and merchandising. He joined the USN July 19, 1968 and served in the USS *Princeton* (LPH-5), Vietnam in 1968.

His memorable experiences include the last part of WESTPAC, Vietnam tour in 1968; Apollo-10 recovery in 1969; Atomic Energy Commission test event in October 1969, Amchitka Island, AK; sharing these experiences with his brother (Brother Duty) and decommissioning of the *Princeton* (Sweet Pea) in 1970. Discharged Dec. 17, 1976.

He is currently owner of Germania auto service. Married to Lois Carryl, he has two children, Stephen Michael and Lisa Ren'ee DePauk-Lebed; and three grandchildren: Justin, Jessica and Cierra.

CLARENCE A. DIETZ, born Sept. 2, 1924 in East Bangor, PA. Inducted April 14, 1943 in the USN and attended seven weeks of boot camp in Sampson, NY. Served as a gunner aboard the USS *Princeton*. His memorable experience was jumping ship when the *Princeton* was sunk during the Pacific Campaign. Sent to Newport, RI and served on the USS *Columbus* until discharged in November 1945 as seaman 1/c.

Retired Dec. 31, 1988 from Dally Slate Company after 35 years. Married to Esther Buzzard, he had five children (one deceased), 11 grandchildren and seven great-grandchildren. Clarence Dietz passed away April 3, 1997 due to heart and lung problems.

BILLY GEORGE EDGIN, born April 10, 1938 in Wichita Falls, TX. He joined the USN Oct. 5, 1955 and served three tours, cruises to the Far East. Discharged April 10, 1959 as BT2.

He was employed in sales with Borden Milk and Ice Cream, retired after 37 years on March 31, 2000. Married to Dorcia Lee, who has been with Avon Products for over 30 years, he has four children: Sherri, Terry, Tina and Mike; eight grandchildren and three great-grandchildren.

RICHARD M. EGRIN, born in Detroit, MI. Graduated from Hillsdale College. He joined the USN and served in Korea, CAG-19-X staff. Retired as commander, USNR.

He is president of Machine R.E. Sales Inc. Married to Estelle, he has two sons, Edward and Stuart; and four grandchildren: Erica, Bradley, Adam and Allison.

RICHMOND R. EMERY, born April 20, 1922 in Elk, WA. Joined the USN (Reserve) in September 1942. Went aboard the USS *Princeton* (CVL-23), October 1943, and the USS *Langley* (CVL-27), February 1945. Served as bombardier gunner VT-23 on 38 combat missions.

Discharged in February 1946 as AFC1/c. Awarded Navy Unit Commendation, Asiatic-Pacific w/8 stars, Air Medal w/7 stars and DFC. He received special recognition Nov. 11, 1997 when selected to the Enlisted Combat Aircrew Roll of Honor (with plaque) aboard the USS *Yorktown* (CV-10), Naval Museum, Mt. Pleasant, SC.

Memorable Experiences: 1) On Feb. 12, 1944 they were on a bombing strike when a piece of shrapnel came through the windshield and lodged in the jaw of Ens. Cox. The blood really gushed out and the whole crew sweated it out until they made an emergency landing and he was rushed to sick bay. 2) two bombing strikes on Truck, April 29, 1944 with very heavy flak and tracer fire all the way to bomb's release; 3) VT-23 aboard USS *Langley* and the night torpedo attack on the Japanese.

Retired as a broker in real estate sales, December 1993. Married to Selma, he has two children, R. Blake and Kristine (married to David Watkins); and five grandchildren: Mathew and Andrew Emery; Katie, Kelsey and Kristian Watkins.

ROBERT WILLIAM "SHORTY" FAHAN, born Oct. 28, 1930 in Norwalk, CT. After attending Norwalk schools, he enlisted in the USN Jan. 28, 1949 and was on active duty until Jan. 27, 1950; recalled Sept. 11, 1950 and proudly served two tours of duty in Korea until 1952 aboard the USS *Princeton* (CV-37).

After being discharged he was designated USNEV, then recalled and discharged June 20, 1953 at the rank of SKG3.

After 42 years with Globe Slicing Machine Co., he and his wife Dorothy relocated to Jupiter, FL where he retired November 1995 from PGA National Resort. He has three children and three grandchildren.

WILLIAM J. FITZGERALD, born June 1, 1938 in Fulton, NY. Joined the USN Nov. 1, 1955. He received an Expeditionary Medal (Taiwan) and was discharged in May 1959 as MM2/c.

Retired November 1994 from Miller Brewery in Fulton, NY. He has five children: William, Kelly, Chris, Robie and David; nine grandchildren.

LELAND R. FLYNN, born Aug. 23, 1932 in Rison, AR. Attended one year of college and three years of business school. Joined the USN in April 1952 and served on the USS *Princeton*, 1953-56. He was assigned to the *Princeton* after Aviation Boatswain's Mate School in Philadelphia, March 1953. About eight weeks later he was high-lined aboard the *Princeton* about 10:00 p.m. off the coast of Korea on a very dark night and dark ship. To get there he took a troop ship from San Francisco to Yokosuka, a two-day train ride to Sasebo, to Korea on three different tankers and one ammo ship and high-lined between ships six times. During this time no pay, no laundry, no haircut. Discharged April 1956 as AB2.

He retired as area manager in Materials Management with GTE in December 1992. Married to Doris and has four children: Brenda, Jima, Terry and Leland Jr.; 19 grandchildren and 10 great-grandchildren.

ROBERT W. FORTWANGLER, born April 15, 1946 in Pittsburgh, PA. Received a BS and MBA. Joined the USN June 14, 1965. Served in Philippines, Okinawa, Sasebo, Japan, Vietnam and Hong Kong. His first encounter of real and extreme poverty was in Olongapol City, PI. Discharged June 7, 1968 as E-4.

He is executive vice-president of Cannon USA. Married to Joyce A., he has three children: Kimberly, Deborah and Robert; and two grandchildren, Robert and McKenzie.

HENRY J. GAAB, enlisted August 1942 in the USN at age 17 and was sent to Great Lakes for gunnery training. Assigned as 20mm gunner to the *Princeton* during construction in Philadelphia and was aboard her until she was sunk in 1944 at Leyte Gulf. While in the water after the sinking, he helped a shipmate in trouble until they were picked up by a whaleboat and put aboard a destroyer (wishes he knew his name and whereabouts). His tour of duty ended September 1945 when discharged from the US Naval Hospital in San Diego, CA.

In 1968 he retired as director of engineering at an Iowa manufacturing company. Married to Eileen for over 57 years, he has three children, five grandchildren and one great-grandson. He returned to Wisconsin in 1983. Due to declining health they enjoy short trips, old friends and especially their family.

HAROLD D. GALLAWAY, born Feb. 5, 1937 in Kansas City, MO. Joined the USN April 19, 1954. When he first saw the *Princeton* his first thought was "Man, you are one big ship" and wondered what adventures laid ahead. He spent 26 months aboard the *Princeton* and two cruises to the Far East. When he was sent to NAS Moffett Field as division petty officer, he knew the real navy was the time spent aboard the *Princeton* and the men of "N" Division. He thought of them as his brothers and to this day he lives in those memories of all they went through - good and bad. Discharged Dec. 4, 1957 as QM3.

Civilian employment as meat cutter and plans to retire June 1, 2002. Married to Muriel, he has two sons, David and Paul.

ALEXANDER "SANDY" GASTON, born Oct. 26, 1946 in New York City, NY. He enlisted in the US Naval Reserve four days after his 17th birthday. While still a high school sophomore, he attended weekly training drills for 37 months, attaining the rank of quartermaster 3/c.

In January 1967 he reported aboard the USS *Princeton* (LPH-5) in Long Beach, CA. Four days later, departed for Vietnam where she participated in combat operations from mid-March until late May when she returned to Long Beach. In late October 1968 he received orders to the USS *Wexford County* (LST-1168).

Discharged Oct. 30, 1969 as QMSN, he was awarded National Defense, Vietnam Service w/4 Bronze Stars, Vietnam Expeditionary Campaign Medal, Combat Action Ribbon and Meritorious Unit Commendation. In June 1996 he was awarded the Meritorious Public Service Citation by USN Secretary John Dalton.

He now self-employed in investments and remains a bachelor with homes in Hawaii and on an island off the coast of Connecticut.

ROBERT CHARLES GIBBON SR., born Jan. 8, 1921 in Philadelphia, PA. Received an ABS degree in 1973 from Lincoln College. He joined the USN on Oct. 15, 1940 and served on the Marianas, Gilberts, Marshalls, Solomons, etc.

He can reflect back and see that there were some good times to remember. Idle time was spent playing cards, reading books or just holding conversation. When he needed to get away, he would go up on the flight deck and watch the planes take-off and land. This was relaxing, somewhat. Looking back, he remembers one night when he was up on the deck and saw this plane coming in; it looked different and sounded different, but he still didn't know what he was in for. Next thing he hears is, "It's a Betty, take

cover." Instinctively, he scampered off, hearing the deck behind him being peppered with gunfire. War was starting to kick in!

After numerous battles and nerve wrecking preparations, the war had taken its toll on this young sailor. This floating city he was on, no longer seemed like the safe haven he had thought it was, call it a sixth sense. His worst fears had come to be a reality, shortly after 1000 Oct. 24, 1944 his life changed forever. A lone enemy bomber hit them with a 500 pound bomb, crippling the *Princeton*, who had achieved so much to this point. When the bomb hit, he was AFT, watching the planes, getting some quality time, but not this time. The bomb penetrated the flight deck, then the hangar deck and finally exploded. There was panic everywhere. Immediately reacting to the situation, he ran toward the elevator well to see what he could do. Things at this point looked grim. Making his way through the dense smoke and panicked stricken sailors, he came across a young man sitting on an equipment locker, scared as hell. He told him to hang on that he would be right back with a life jacket and to stay where he was. When he reached the upper deck, the order "abandon ship" was issued. He hesitated thinking of what he should do. The inevitable was there, he had to jump. Luckily a friend of his, Johnny D'Andrea had given him his Mae West when he returned Stateside due to a medical mishap. He thought he was somewhat prepared. Upon hitting the water, thoughts began to race through his mind. What about the other men on the ship? Was he going to live? Would he live to see his family again? THE KID! He hoped that kid didn't wait for him.

The seas were rough that day, he remembers bobbing up and down, waves to big for him to guess, and watching his ship being destroyed in slow motion. The waves would take him up. He could see the tragic *Princeton* in its last hours and when the waves would go down, all he could see was nothing but rough ocean waters in front of him. After nearly two hours, the *Gatling* finally came to their rescue. They dropped a cargo net down for them to climb, it took him two tries to finally scale that net. Upon reaching the deck he thanked the Lord for returning him to safe ground and kissed the deck. Later he met up with one of his good friends, Ernie McGill, who also was on the ship, and Robert kissed him too!

A lot has happened over the last 57 years, but he will never forget Oct. 24, 1944. He still suffers from battle fatigue, but thanks God that he was there to serve this wonderful country.

Discharged Oct. 14, 1945 as aviation machinist's mate 1/c and awarded nine Battle Stars.

Retired from civilian employment in 1982. Married Jennie Ruoff and has three children: Jennie, Robert Jr. and Richard; five grandchildren: Robert III, Christopher, Andrew, Audrey and Kelly and two great-grandchildren, Barry and Lydia.

DAVID S. GRAY, born April 15, 1930 in LaCrosse, WI. Received a BA from DePauw University. He served in the USN Sept. 6, 1951 to March 19, 1952 and joined the Reserves March 20, 1952.

Participated in two Korean cruises aboard the USS *Princeton*, April-October 1952 and March-July 1953. He received the Korean Service Medal, UN Medal, National Defense Medal and Navy Unit Commendation. Discharged Feb. 25, 1955 as lieutenant junior grade and resigned April 13, 1966.

He retired as manager of Field Operations - Census 2000 on Sept. 15, 2000.

Married Janice Nov. 15, 1952 and has three children: Stephen, Alan and Lisa, and eight grandchildren.

JACK J. GREGG (AKA ALVIN CLYDE GREGG JR.), born June 11, 1939 in Navasota, Grimes County, TX. Received a GED from Alvin Junior College May 14, 1971 and attended Law Enforcement Basic Certification Course April 1972.

Joined the USN in 1956 and served in the Far East, assigned to 4th Division of Gunnery. Discharged Nov. 13, 1962 as seaman.

Employed by Alvin Police Dept., 1971-73; Pearland Police Dept., 1973-74; Webster Police Dept., 1974-77; Lake Jackson Police Dept., 1977-82; Boerne Police Dept., 1982-83; Kendall County Sheriff Dept., 1983-86; Boerne Police Dept., 1986-1990 and Kendall County Sheriff Dept., 1990 to present as command sergeant. He was elected Kendall County Constable, Precinct 4, Jan. 1, 2001.

Married to Geri and has children from first marriage, Melody; second marriage: Sophia, Jack Jr., David, Gene, Stephanie; third marriage: Melanie, Jennifer, Joy, Kris and Scott; and 24 grandchildren.

LEE R. HAHNE, born Oct. 8, 1944 in Washington, MO. Graduated high school and went to Trade School for millwright trade. Joined the US Marine Corps Dec. 1, 1961. From September-December 1962 he served on a three-month cruise to the Johnson Islands where the government did testing of nuclear bombs and participated in WESTPAC cruise from February-November 1963 as command ship for Task Group 76.5. He was discharged Nov. 30, 1964.

Retired from Chrysler Corporation in 1992. He has three sons: Steve, Jeff and Chris; two granddaughters, Jessica and Sarah.

EDWARD L. HAMILTON, enlisted in the USN Jan. 5, 1955. He was assigned to the USS *Princeton* and served with her until his discharge in 1958. He was in the V6 Division with a great bunch of guys.

He went with United Airlines (ground crew) for 10 years, then became an engineering inspector until retirement in 1998. He met his wife Geraldine two months after his discharge from the USN and they married two years later. They have three children: Patricia, Mary and Edward Jr., sons-in-law, Mark and Peter; daughter-in-law Beverly; five grandchildren: Sean, Nikke, Ethan, Lauren and Simon. His family and the ship are the biggest part of his life.

One thing he learned aboard the "Sweet P" was to love and protect what he has. He would love to hear from the guys of V6 Division. They can contact him through the USS Princeton Veterans, Inc.

DUANE L. HELLER, born Aug. 5, 1933 in Oxford, NE. Graduated high school and attended two years of college. He joined the USN July 10, 1952 in Helmer, IN. Served on the USS *Princeton* (CVA-37) in 1953, Task Force 77 in Korea and 1954-56 on USS *Princeton* (CVS-37), anti-submarine maneuvers.

His memorable experiences include Electronics School at Treasure Island, San Francisco, CA; escort for Japanese orphans at 1954 Christmas party on board the USS *Princeton* in Yokosuka, Japan; and visits to Formosa, Hong Kong, Okinawa, Thailand, Hawaii and Japan. Discharged July 5, 1956 as ETR1.

He retired February 1995 as a plant engineer. Married to Rita, he has three daughters and two grandchildren.

JOHN P. HENRY JR., born May 28, 1931 in Erie, PA. Graduated high school in East Brady, PA and attended Grove City College, Grove City, PA as business major. He joined the USN Jan. 21, 1951 in Pittsburgh, PA. Attended boot camp at Great Lakes, IL with Co. 231 and Aviation Ordnance School in Jacksonville April 26, 1951.

Reported aboard the USS *Princeton* Oct. 27, 1951 at Bremerton, WA. Joined Task Force 77 off Korea April-October 1952; rejoined Task Force 77 off Korea March 13, 1953 before the Korean Armistice was signed July 27, 1953. He transferred to VF-152 Moffett Field, CA Nov. 5, 1953 and went aboard USS *Yorktown* (CV-10) June 11, 1954, headed for the States. Discharged from Treasure Island Dec. 14, 1954 with rank AO3.

He retired from Cigna Insurance Co. in May 1986 after 28 years. Enjoys hunting, fishing and is a member of VFW Post 8803. Married to Mary Jane, he has four step-children and nine step-grandchildren.

WILLIAM RONALD HENSLEY, ADRC, born Aug. 3, 1937 in Asheville, NC. Attended some college and joined the USN. Served in Vietnam aboard the USS *Boxer* (LPH-4). Late in 1955 and most of 1956 he was aboard the *Princeton* (CVS-37) for WESTPAC cruise, a member of VS-20 based at NAAS Brownsfield. Some of his shipmates were Fredrick Austin Cimino, Leroy J. "Lee" Dautreuil, Roger G. Menk and Clyde B. Tiffany. Discharged Sept. 27, 1974 as chief petty officer.

Retired Sept. 30, 1999 as mayor of Bruce, MS. Married Dorothy and has grandchildren: William and Jenna Hensley; Ashley, Tony and Sydney Kate Mask.

May God Bless all the line crew of VS-20. Anyone who would care to write can reach me at PO Box 481, Bruce, MS 38915.

MARTIN F. HERBERT, born March 4, 1932 in Macedonia, IA. Graduated Macedonia High School and attended Iowa State University for one year following USN discharged. He joined the USN, O-I Division in May 1951. Served with Task Force 77 during Korean Conflict, participated in 3-1/2 cruises and flew back to the US from Japan on the last cruise.

Memorable experiences include two visits to Hong Kong on two different cruises and being able to serve with his brother, Leo F. Herbert, in the O-I division on the last 2-1/2 cruises. Discharged April 1955 as RD2.

He retired Dec. 1, 1992 after 34 years with Omaha Public Power District. Married to Beverly for over 44 years, they have four children: Angela, Melanie, Chris and Michael; three granddaughters and three grandsons.

WILLIAM J. "WILL" HICKMAN, born Oct. 16, 1927. He received BS and master's degree from George Washington University. Joined the USN in 1944 and served in WWII, Korea and Vietnam. He served on the USS *Princeton* as a pilot and performed 100 landings. Discharged in 1984 as captain.

He was married to Margaret and had three children and two grandchildren. William Hickman passed away Sept. 4, 1998.

JERROLD J. "JAKE" HIGGINBOTHAM, born June 5, 1941 in Salem, OR. Attended and graduated from Columbia Christian High School, Portland, OR in 1960. Enlisted in the USMC in October the same year. Attended basic training at MCRD, San Diego, CA and assigned his first duty as ships company, USS *Princeton* (LPH-5) in 1961 as private E-1.

Served in the Marine Guard and later in commissary (cook's section), "I ate well aboard ship." He left the "Sweet P" in 1963 as corporal E-4 and transferred back to MCRD, San Diego, CA.

Returned to Oregon and married Nancy J. Fuller from Parkrose, OR in 1964. He is blessed with three children: Jerry, Ronald and Stacy; two granddaughters, Katlin, Jessy with a third on the way.

In 1967 he fulfilled a lifelong ambition to work in the field of law enforcement, attended Oregon State Police Academy and was appointed a police officer that same year. He retired from police work in 1997.

In 1974 he joined the Oregon Army National Guard, obtained and retired with the rank of E-7, sergeant first class at age 60.

GEORGE L. HIGGINSON, born Sept. 25, 1924 in Kinmundy, IL. Graduated Indiana State Teachers College in August 1950. Joined the USN in August 1942 and was discharged January 1946 as radioman 2/c. He was recalled in April 1951 and discharged again in March 1953 as radioman 2/c. Served his entire tour in CVL-23 and USS LST 920 during WWII and in CV-37 in Korea.

He was employed as division chief underwriter at Liberty Mutual Insurance Co. Married to Rosemary H. Rieschel, he had four children: Mary Lou, Beverly Ann, Jeffrey Lawrence and Janet Elizabeth; two grandchildren, Samantha Leigh and Christina Elizabeth. George Higginson passed away Sept. 27, 1976 from a heart attack.

George Higginson was my dad. When he died, I was barely 17, my sisters and brother were in grade school. He never told us very much about his Navy days, so if any of his shipmates remember either his CVL-23 days (he was aboard for her entire tour of duty) or his CV-37 days (attached to the admiral's staff), we would love to hear from you. Please contact Mary Lou Shea, 9 Bromfield St., Quincy, MA 02170 or by e-mail shead@enc.edu.

MICHAEL D. "MIKE" HILL, born May 22, 1942 in Wichita, KS. Received a BS from Wichita State University in 1978. He joined the USN on Nov. 17 1959 and served on the USS *Princeton* (LPH-5). Participated in Operation Dominic on Midway Island, Spring/Summer 1962; LPH5, February 1962-March 1963 and in Armed Forces Radio/TV. Discharged April 30, 1963 and from inactive Reserves on Nov. 17, 1965.

Employed as police officer with the Wichita Police Dept. in July 1963, moving up the ranks to Commander Special Investigations in January 1985, then Sedgwick County Sheriff from 1985-2001. He retired after 37 years of diversified responsibility in law enforcement and government operations. He is a member of the American Legion and active in numerous community activities. Married to Judy and has a stepson, Blake Ellis.

JAMES A. HUNNICUTT, born Sept. 10, 1914 in Klamath Falls, OR. Attended courses at Contra Costa Junior College. He joined the USNR and served in the Aleutian Islands, South Pacific and the Battle of Leyte Gulf. Discharged Aug. 8, 1945 as chief quartermaster and awarded Silver Star, Purple Heart, Philippine Liberation Ribbon and Philippine Republic Presidential Unit Citation.

Dora Jane Bowen and Jim met shortly after Pearl Harbor. He had enlisted and was on his way to the Naval Station in San Diego, CA, and they got on the same train. She was on her way to Berkeley and he asked for her address since he had no one to correspond with (she found out later he had a wonderful family in Oregon). Three of his brothers were in the Navy and two in the Army - this was revealed as they corresponded. At first, Dora was a student at UC Berkeley then joined the Army one month after she graduated, age 21. When the news came of the *Princeton's* sinking, Jim's sister called Dora to tell her he was one of the survivors. Jim told her later that he saw the Japanese pilot who dropped the bomb and started the fatal fire and explosion that eventually sunk the ship. Although wounded, he stayed to fight fire and save those trapped below. He never could get rid of the horrible memory of the cruiser *Birmingham's* bulkhead that bore the bloody imprint of bodies.

He returned home to San Francisco, married Dora at City Hall, returned to the Pentagon and reported to Corpus Christi. During the last days of the war he helped to sell War Bonds by radio and by visits (one to Mexico). After the war, he became a cabinet maker and wonderfully encouraged Dora in her college teaching career. They had one great son and two wonderful grandchildren. He had a great variety in his lifetime, sheep herding for a Basque, logging and heavy equipment operator, building, fishing and camping. James Hunnicutt passed away January 1987.

RICHARD MONTGOMERY JACKSON, born Dec. 9, 1920 in Jacksonville, FL. Received a BS from Harvard in 1942. Served as lieutenant commander in USN Reserves during WWII. The USS *Princeton* (CVL-23) was commissioned Feb. 25, 1943 in Philadelphia, PA and departed June 1, 1943 for Trinidad to train all hands for the many battles they were soon to be engaged. Received a star for each of the following operations: Pacific Raids, Treasury-Bougainville, Gilbert Island, Marshall Island, Asiatic-Pacific Raids, Hollandia, Marianas, Western Caroline Island and Leyte.

A former airline executive, he married Martha Eustis Turner Sept. 12, 1942 and has three children: Richard, Susanne (Mrs. Jeffrey Miller) and William.

RICHARD EARL KAGY, born June 1, 1931 in Olney, IL. Joined the USN June 14, 1949 and served with Task Force 77 in Korea and in Guam.

His memorable experiences include: two major campaigns, Task Force 77 in 1952, 500 US planes knocked out five Big Red power plants in heaviest raid in Korea; 850 planes blasted Red Korea supply center in biggest air raid of war; when the *Princeton* collided with a tanker during refueling; hitting two major typhoons, Karen and Mary, one was 72 knots; and during replenishment in Sea of Japan, Cdr. Dr. Snowden performed hernia surgery on him. Also memorable was in the 1970s when his son lucky enough to serve in the *J.F. Kennedy* and they got to take a tour. He also served on the USS *Enterprise*.

Discharged June 13, 1953, ship service man 3/c.

He retired April 1, 1987 from Granite City Steel (National) as caster foreman. Married to Donna, he has two sons, Richard Jr. and Ronald; five grandchildren: Carrie, Natalie, Nick, Mike and Jenny; three great-grandchildren: Adrianne, Jasmine and Jordan.

GAIL E. KEITH, born July 8, 1944 in Florence, CO. Attended two years college. He joined the USN in January 1962. Served two tours in Vietnam (Chu Lai, Saigon) and Delta AROA and one tour at Johnson Island. Discharged in April 1968 as BT2.

Retired in November 1999 from Montana Highway Patrol after 30 years. Currently he is an investigator for Montana Board of Outfitters.

Married to Linda, he has three children: Gail Jr., Bart and Lath; four grandchildren: Payton, Dylan, Kody and Genises.

GEORGE RICHARD KOLAR, born March 2, 1928 in Cicero, IL. Attended Electrical Trade School and enlisted in the Naval Reserve Dec. 3, 1947. Studied to become an electrician's mate. Had cruises on Lake Michigan aboard USN PC and PCE's. Promoted to fireman March 1950 and called to active duty Aug. 10, 1950. Spent 10 days at the Great Lakes Training Center prior to departing for Bremerton, WA where he boarded the USS *Princeton* and became a plankowner.

Civilian job was as an electrical helper but he was assigned to the boiler room; after six months he transferred to the E Div. Aboard ship he made two trips into Korean waters with stops in both Hawaii and Japan for R&R.

His four-year enlistment was extended, due to the war, to five years. Discharged Dec. 2, 1952 as EMP3 and awarded Combat Action Ribbon, Navy Unit Commendation Ribbon, ROK Presidential Unit Citation, National Defense Service Ribbon, Korean Service w/Battle Stars, UN Korean Service Medal and Navy Occupation Medal.

He retired from the electrical union in 1973 and went to work for the Village of La Grange Park as building and electrical inspector. Retired in 1996 and currently living in La Grange, IL.

Married to Charlotte Kostka in June 1950 (divorced), he has two children, George and Cathy; two grandchildren, Geoffrey and Katherine.

GEORGE W. KNOTT, Master Gunnery Sergeant, enlisted in the US Marine Corps in 1949 at age 17. After spending time in Korea, the Mediterranean and several Stateside bases he was assigned to the USS *Princeton* (LPH-5) in 1959. One day while the *Princeton* was docked at Pier Echo in Long Beach, CA, the ship's commanding officer, Capt. Brower announced that there would be a Dependence Day Cruise Aug. 15, 1960. Military personnel were permitted to invite one civilian on board. On the cruise, a fellow *Princeton* Marine, Bob Fling and his wife Donna, introduced him to their friend, Marjorie.

The day's activities were a ship's tour out into the harbor, lunch and an airshow observing helicopter operations. At the end of the day they were given liberty. That evening, Marjorie and he went with their *Princeton* Marine friends to a night club dancing. Six weeks later he proposed.

They were married Nov. 10, 1960 on the Marine Corps birthday. After their ceremony, Marjorie and he went to the *Princeton's* Marine Corps Ball in the Hilton Hotel Ballroom in Long Beach. Nov. 10, 2000 they celebrated 40 years of marriage.

PAUL F. KREIE, born Oct. 17, 1925 in Brantford, ND. He joined the USN before graduating from high school in 1942. He was stationed in the Pacific and discharged in February 1946 as S1.

He retired at age 61 after 39 years of employment as a welder for the Burlington Northern Railroad.

Married Shirley Blomquist on May 25, 1955 (deceased April 2000) and has two children, Paulette (Mrs. Bruce Whitmore) and Brian; two grandchildren, Jenessa and Kira Whitmore.

JAMES H. LOVE SR., boarded *"Sweet Pea"* in November 1964 at sea. He was fortunate enough to climb up her side. An E-2 when first assigned to her, he stood messenger watch in aft engine room. During his tour he advanced to E-5 standing underway top watch, both upper and lower level of aft engine room. He was in charge of the generator gang and aft engine room repairs. He had the good fortune to serve with many good machinist mates, especially Dale Chaney MM3, Bobby Johnson MM2 and Kurt Oleson MM3. He left the *Sweet Pea* in August 1968 in Da Nang.

JOHN HANS MALMEN, born Nov. 9, 1925 in Chicago, IL. Attended Venice High School, Los Angeles, CA. Joined the USN on Nov. 9, 1942. He boarded the USS *Princeton* at Philadelphia Navy Yard in March 1943. She was his ship from the time she left for the Pacific on July 21, 1943 until she was sunk Oct. 24, 1944.

He was on duty during every battle and campaign: Occupation of Baker Island, raids on Tarawa and Makin Island, Buka Bonis Strike, Rabaul Strike, Nauru Island Strike, Gilbert Island Operation, Occupation of Kwajalein and Majuro Atolls, Occupation of Eniwetok Atoll; Palau, Yap, Ulithi, Woleai Raids; Occupation of Hollandia, New Guinea; Truk, Satawan, Ponape Raids; neutralization of Japanese bases in the Marianas and Western Pacific; capture and occupation of Saipan; Battle of the Philippine Sea; capture and occupation of Guam and Tinian; Occupation of Peleliu and Anguar, Palau Island; strikes on Mindanao, Central Philippine Islands, Manila, Luzon, Visayas, Nasei Shoto, Formosa; second battle of the Philippine Sea and sinking of the USS *Princeton*.

He was commended by the commanding officer, USN for Meritorious Conduct while serving on the USS *Princeton* during operations against the enemy. Discharged Jan. 11, 1947 as watertender 2/c.

Retired in December 1975 as fire management officer, US Forest Service, Hat Creek District of Lassen National Forest, Fall River Mills, CA. Married Janice Kohl on May 14, 1955 and has three sons: John, Joel and James; and two grandchildren, Jonathan and Nicole.

HARRY MARCHESINI, born Jan. 8, 1927 in Fredericktown, PA. Attended one year of college. He joined the USN Jan. 1, 1944 and served on the USS *Princeton* (CV-23) May-October 1944. Discharged March 25, 1965 as PT1.

Retired from civilian employment on Jan. 26, 1992. Married Anna Mae Magda and has three children: William J. Ferencak III, Colette Pollock and Claudette Clapper; and two grandchildren, Hilary and William Ferencak IV.

MICHAEL J. MASSA, born June 1945 in Omaha, NE, reared and schooled in Sturgis, SD. He joined the USN in August 1962 and attended boot camp in San Diego. First duty station at NAD Concord, CA aboard YTM-180 *Madokawando*.

Reported to *Princeton* (LPH-5) in December 1963 and spent time in the 2nd, 1st and 3rd Divisions. He was petty officer in charge of the 2nd Division in 1966. Served on *Princeton* for operations Jackstay, Osage, Deckhouse 1, Nathan Hale, Deckhouse 2 and Hastings. Discharged August 1966 as boatswain's mate 2/c.

He attended the University of South Dakota and was a resort/restaurant owner until selling it in 1995. Married to Jan, he has three children: Jake, Ann and Josh.

JOSEPH E. MCARDLE, born April 17, 1927 in Syracuse, NY. He joined the USN on Nov. 9, 1943 and left boot camp Jan. 6, 1944 assigned to the USS *Princeton*. Participated in the Battle of Leyte Gulf where the ship sank and returned to Philadelphia, PA. Assigned to advanced training base in Bizerte, Tunisia where he was trained on radio controlled boats to be sent in for demolition purposes. Assigned to USS LCI 9445 and participated in the Battle of Southern France and returned to Newport, RI for advanced training. He was then assigned to the new USS *Princeton* (CV-37) for shakedown cruise.

He recalls while performing his duty on the captain's gig, he went to Capt. Hoskins bachelor's quarters to get his gear. Capt. Hoskins told him not to forget the package in the corner and to be careful of it, as it was his "extra leg." Discharged April 19, 1946 as coxswain.

He retired Feb. 3, 1983 as a firefighter for the city of Syracuse. Married to Mary S., his children and stepchildren are: Joseph E. Jr., Pauline, Cheryl, John and Nancy Black. He has 14 grandchildren and four great-grandchildren.

ELBERT W. MCRAE, born July 31, 1929 in Zena, OK. He joined the USN on June 30, 1948. Served with the USS *Rendova* (CVE-114) in Korea with Marine Fighter Squadron VMF-212, Flying Cosairs; USS *Princeton* (CVS-37) in late 1953 until 1957 and USN Recruiting Station, Topeka, KS 1957-61.

He rejoined the fleet onboard USS *Gunston Hall* (LSD-5). During the Cuban Missile Crisis in 1963 he became a destroyer sailor reporting on board USS *Duncan* (DDR-874), USS *Ingersoll* (DD-652), USS *Perkins* DD-877 and USS *Parsons* DD-949.

In 1964 he returned to Fort Smith, AR for more recruiting duty. In 1967 he returned to sea duty reporting to USS *Pawcatuck* (AD-108) in Loraine, OH for modernization. Transitioned from St. Lawrence seaway to Boston Navy Yard. He retired from this ship Jan. 8, 1968 as E-6 SH1 after 20 years service.

While on board USS *Rendova* (CVE-114) he participated in first hydrogen bomb test at Eniwetok, South Pacific, Operation Ivy, becoming a test participate and a downwinder.

He retired from the US Post Office in Miami, OK July 31, 1986. His total government service was 38-1/2 years. Married to Betty A. Beach for over 47 years, he has five children: Malcolm, Everet, Jane, Karen and James; nine grandchildren: William and Scott Snider; Suzzane and John McRae; Laura Henderson; Jessica Dodson; Stephen, Brandon and Brittany McRae; and one great-granddaughter, Elizabeth Snider.

CYRUS T. MICHAEL, born Jan. 7, 1924 in Crawfordsville, IN. Received an AA degree from Maricopa Technical College. He joined the USN in August 1941. Overseas stations included: USS *Salt Lake City* (CA-25), USS *Salamaua* (CVE-96), USS *Douglas H. Fox* (DD-779), USS *Herbert J. Thomas* (DD-833), USS *The Sullivans* (DD-537), USS *William T. Powell* (DER-213) and USS *Princeton* (CV-37 and LPH-5).

He participated in Marcus Island raid, Guadalcanal-Tulagi landings, Battle of Cape

Esperance, Tarawa Island, Battle of Komandorskie Island, Occupation of Attu, Gilbert Islands Operation, escort for Doolittle Raid on Tokyo, Okinawa Gunto picket line and Korea's East Coast support for forces at Pohang. Retired from the service July 1961 as B/T/C.

After 19-1/2 years as custodian for the Washington School District, he retired January 1985. Married to May, he has three children: Walter, Priscilla and Susan; nine grandchildren and two great-granddaughters.

SAM A. MILLER, born Jan. 12, 1917 in Monticello, NY. Graduated from Honolulu High School. He joined the USN in mid-1930s. Overseas stations included: Ford Island, Pearl Harbor; French Morocco, Africa and John Rogers NAS Hawaii. Ships served on: USS *Texas* (BB-35), USS *Ranger* (CA-4), USS *Sangamon* (CVE-26), USS *Princeton* (CV-23), USS *Hornet* (CV-12) and USS *Leyte* (CV-32).

Shipmates Chief John Face and Leo Keri (both deceased) served with him on USS *Sangamon* and USS *Princeton*. Participated in invasion of North Africa, Battle of the Philippine Sea and invasion of the Mariana Islands. He flew as a dive bomber gunner until 1944 and then as torpedo plane turret gunner on missions against the Marianas, Philippines, Iwo Jima, etc. He was in every theater of war except CBI. Retired as chief aviation machinist mate in mid-1950s, awarded DFC and Air Medal w/3 Gold Stars.

He was married to Opal Greer of Kentucky and Emiko Yatsugi of Japan, both are deceased.

LEO C. NASSER, born Nov. 29, 1937 in Covina, CA. Joined the USN in Jan. 17, 1955 and was discharged in 1958. He received a BS and is employed with Scott Engineering. Married to Patricia, he has three children: Joy, Jana and Scott; and one grandson, Drake Wallace.

JERRY NEMEROVSKY, born March 22, 1934 in Cleveland, OH. Enlisted in the USN on Aug. 7, 1951 and took his physical in Detroit, MI. From there he was sent to Great Lakes for 11 weeks of wisdom. Assigned to the *Princeton*, R Division as a pipefitter. R&R was one of his favorite times. He went once to Fuji New Grand Hotel and once to Fuji View Hotel on Lake Yamanaka at the bottom of Mt. Fuji. He also thought liberties in Japan were cool.

After he came up for discharge, the fun began. He was still over in the Sea of Japan so they transferred him to a destroyer by high-line. The ship had a change of orders so they transferred him again by high-line to another ship and ended up in Sasebo, Japan. He spent two days on a train to Tokyo to catch a plane to Hawaii; then to Treasure Island, CA for discharge two weeks past his date. Discharged April 4, 1955 as FPFN and awarded National Defense, Korean PUC, Navy Commendation, Korean Service and United Nations Medal.

He attended Barber college and owned his own shop until he retired March 20, 2000 after 40 years. Married to Jerry, he has six children and 14 grandchildren.

J.C. OTIS, born Sept. 21, 1922 in Butler Township, MI. The youngest son of 11 children, J.C. (nicknamed Connie) graduated from Quincy High School in June 1942. Upon graduation he wasted no time in joining the war effort.

He was sworn into the USNR November 1942 and was assigned to USNTS, Great Lakes, IL. Upon completion of training he was assigned to the USS *Princeton* Jan. 30, 1943 and boarded February 25. Connie served on the *Princeton* until its demise October 1944 and was then assigned to Bunker Hill USNAS in Indiana until October 1945 when he was reassigned to NAS Memphis, TN. After his discharge Feb. 27, 1946, he returned to Quincy, MI and married Dorothy Barnett from Ann Arbor, MI.

To this union was born one son and five girls, one whom died in infancy. He worked at Homer Furnace and later for many years at Foundry Material Corp. in Coldwater, MI until retirement December 1981. Reared in the country, he had a lifelong love of hunting and fishing. After learning of the *Princeton* reunions he was able to attend nine and always looked forward to seeing his old shipmates.

Sadly, Connie passed away April 11, 1994 leaving his wife Dorothy, five children, 12 grandchildren and 18 great-grandchildren.

DEWEY SHADWICK PARKER, born April 7, 1924 in Monte Lake, TN. Attended Technical School. He joined the USN on May 17, 1943. Stationed on USS *Princeton* he participated in Pacific Raids of 1943, New Guinea Operation (Hollandia), Treasury-Bougainville Operation, Gilbert Island Operation, Marshall Island Operation, Asiatic-Pacific Raids of 1944 and Western Pacific-East Coast of Luzon-Philippine Islands.

He recalls a Japanese plane flew between the *Birmingham* and the *Princeton*. The gun emplacements on the flight deck of the aircraft carrier were mounted high and the cruiser's guns were low. Both opened fire at the same time. He and a shipmate observed that the plane seemed out of control, the pilot was injured or dead wearing a red scarf around his neck. His shipmate said it wasn't a scarf, but appeared to be blood. The plane crashed in the water just pass the bow of the *Birmingham* and *Princeton*.

On October 24, a lone fighter bomber hit the portside of the flight deck of the *Princeton* and traveled through a parked TBF bomber, then continued through the hangar deck and exploded in the galley. He found his way to the flight deck to help the crew clear the deck of planes. The ship was burning at portend and they could hear explosions. When "abandon ship" was sounded he slid down a line to the water and swam to the destroyer *Irwin* to a cargo net and climbed aboard. Discharged Dec. 7, 1945 as aviation machinist mate 3/c SV-6, petty officer, flight deck plane captain.

He retired July 1, 1998 as a federal coalmine inspector with the Department of Labor.

Married to Elizabeth, he has three children: Carrie Lee Kincaid, Dr. Bill Parker and Nancy Campbell; nine grandchildren: Phillip, John and Rebecca Kincaid; Amanda Oaks; Shannon, Aubrey and Seth Parker; William and Patrick Campbell; and four great-grandchildren: Jacob, Casey, Shelby and Whitney Kincaid.

SEYMOUR PARSONS, born July 5, 1916 in Chicago, IL. Graduated from Yale University and entered the Navy Reserve in August 1941. He served as the radar specialist officer on the *Princeton* (CVL-23) and was a plankowner from the February 1943 commissioning until the ship was sunk in October 1944. Transferred to the Retired Reserve June 1, 1954 with the rank of lieutenant commander.

He was a senior analytical engineer with Hamilton Standard, a division of United Technologies from April 1946 to July 1977. Supervised a group specialized in developing computer analyses to determine vibratory stresses in aircraft propellers. He and his wife, Christina, now deceased, had three children: Julie, Ben and Kristin; and two granddaughters.

CLARENCE EDWIN PEEL, born Jan. 12, 1919 in Perry, Dallas County, IA. Graduated from Perry High School in 1937. He joined the USN in December 1941. Served at NAS in Willow Grove, PA; Jacksonville, FL (participated as a Navy boxer); Great Lakes, IL; Norfolk, VA and San Diego, CA. Traveled aboard the aircraft carriers USS *Cowpens,* USS *Wasp* and USS *Princeton.* Participated in the Mariana Turkey Shoot and was at Eniwetok for the A-bomb test.

In 1950 he joined the crew of the USS *Princeton* for service in the Korean War. All of his Navy memories are memorable. Discharged June 1980 as aviation ordnanceman 1/c with a total of 30 years of Naval Reserve and active time.

He retired June 1, 1985 as plant operator at Perry Municipal Water Works.

Married to Lois, he has one daughter, Verah (Mrs. Richard Peddicord); a grandson Richard married to Shannan Howell and two great-grandsons, Sinjin Dakota and Tyler Reese.

RONALD O. PEERS, born in Chicago, IL. Joined the USN in October 1948 during the 1948 Berlin Airlift Crisis for one year active service and seven years Reserve. He was called back to active service in July 1950 and helped get the *Princeton* out of mothballs.

Served on the USS *Worcester* (CL-144), USS *Newport News* (CA-148) and the USS *Princeton* (CV-37). Discharged October 1953 and awarded Letter of Commendation (earned on *Princeton*), Korean Service Medal, United Nations Medal, American Defense Medal, Navy Asian Occupation Medal and Korean Presidential Unit Citation Ribbon.

Retired from US Banknote Corp. in 1993 where he worked in the composing room, eventually becoming department superintendent. Enjoys retirement and is a member of VFW Post 3579.

Married to Dolores, he has two children, David and Donna (married to Norman); two grandsons, Kevin and Ryan.

MAX E. PETERSON, born June 5, 1931 in Ottawa, KS. Received a BSEE from Colorado University and a MSEE from Southern Methodist University. He joined the USN on Jan. 24, 1951. Served on the USS *Princeton* in 1952-53 on the Korean Cruise. One of his memorable experiences was spending time on vultures row watching air operations. Discharged Dec. 17, 1954 as ET1.

He retired Aug. 31, 1993 from Alcatel, nee Rockwell, nee Collins Radio after 34 years. Married to the former Jania D. Scribner, he has two children, Mark Allen and Julie Helen; and two granddaughters, Nicole and Jaimie.

BUFORD JORDAN POLLETT, born in Johnson County, GA. Graduated in 1952 from Wrightsville High School. He joined the USN on July 9, 1952 and participated in overseas campaigns until truce with North Korea was signed in February 1953. He recalls working to save pilots when their planes crashed on the flight deck and putting out the fires. Discharged July 9, 1956 as AB3.

He retired in 1996 from Fortsman's Textile Co. Married to Mary Elizabeth and has a son Buford Boyd.

CHARLES L. PRYOR, born Dec. 24, 1928 in Caldwell, KS. Graduated from Caldwell High School in May 1946 and received an associate's degree from Arkansas City (Kansas) Junior College in May 1954; a BS from Phillips University, Enid, OK in May 1956 in accounting and business administration.

He joined the USN on May 29, 1946 and was assigned to USS *Wilksbarrie* (CL-103). Served until 1948 in European Theater of Operations. Recalled to active duty July 1951 and served aboard the USS *Princeton* in Korea until March 1953. Released to inactive Reserves until July 1954 and received two Bronze Battle Stars. Discharged in July 1954 as SKG-T 2/c.

He served as senior contract administrator with Unisys Corp. under a NASA contract with Rockwell Corp. with the space shuttle program at Johnson Space Center, Houston, TN. Retired Feb. 15, 1991. Married to Beverly Ann, he has a son, Charles II who lives in Berkeley, CA.

E.B. "BUZZ" PURCELL JR., born May 28, 1925 in Newberry, SC. Graduated from The Citadel and University of South Carolina Law School. He joined the USN in August 1943 and served as a pilot in VF-152 aboard the USS *Princeton* during the Korean War.

On March 22, 1953 while flying as a pilot in VF-152 and attacking (dive bombing and strafing) a North Korean target, he encountered anti-aircraft fire that raked up the left side of his F-4U Corsair with a piece of flak lodging in his left arm. He immediately set about getting a tourniquet on his arm and inhaled some smelling salts. LTJG Denny Joiner radioed him to follow him to the nearest South Korean airfield (K-18) for landing. The hydraulic system was shot out and he had to use the emergency CO2 system to get the landing gear down. The throttle linkage was frozen so he had to turn off the engine switch and make a dead stick landing. An Air Force doctor at K-18 treated his wound temporarily and he was returned to the *Princeton* via the back seat of an A D Skyraider flown by Lt. A.C. Dinnel of VA-155. Dr. Jim Barnett, the CAG 15 Flight Surgeon, treated his arm until it healed.

On May 3, 1953 he encountered anti-aircraft fire that was a direct hit to his engine, knocking it completely out. He was able to glide to the ocean and ditched his Corsair about half mile from shore. Picked up by a Navy helicopter (a Sikorski HU1) and flown to its homebase aboard LST-735 anchored in Wonson Harbor. The crewman of the helicopter was R.L. Welch, AD2 and the pilot turned out to be an old friend LCDR Don L. Good. The exposure "poopy" suit provided protection from the cold temperature of the water about 30 minutes. Fortunately he had no injuries. After returning to the *Princeton* via the *St. Paul* and a destroyer, he learned that two squadron mates from VF-152, Ens. Malcolm Quinley and Lt. Lee Richey, his roommate, had been shot down and lost as a result of anti-aircraft fire. He was discharged in April 1958 as lieutenant commander.

Retired from practicing law in 1989. Married to Ann, he has two children, Mary Ann Ridgeway and E.B. III.

JAMES LEWIS RABOURN, born Jan. 3, 1916 in Carrier Mills, IL. Attended Southern Illinois University for one year in 1937 and joined the USN on Sept. 9, 1937. He was assigned to the USS *Chicago* (CA-29) in 1938 (basketball champions that year). Attended Navy Gun Fire Control School, Gun Control Computer School, Sperry Gyroscope School, 40mm Electric-Hydraulic Gun Power Drive School and Navy Fire Fighting School. Pre-commission to USS *Princeton* (CVL-23) as chief gunfire control.

He had overseas duty on USS *Princeton* to February 1944, temporary commission naval officer and transfer to USS *Springfield* (CL-66). Resigned as lieutenant junior grade Jan. 15, 1946. Joined the Naval Reserve April 2, 1947 and retired July 1, 1962 as lieutenant commander after 21 years. Awarded American Defense w/star, American Theater, APCM w/7 stars, Good Conduct Medal w/star, Philippine, WWII VM, China Service, Naval Reserve, Naval Cruiser "Ironman Medal."

Memorable experience was taking off in a torpedo bomber from the deck of the USS *Princeton*; ordering more torpedoes for the ship and shooting down a Japanese bomber from fantail 40mm mount.

He joined the Naval Hospital, Corona, CA Fire Department in 1946. In 1952 the hospital closed and became the Naval Weapon Station. He retired as fire chief June 15, 1973.

Married Grace Elizabeth Cooper January 1940 and has a daughter, Cynthia Hendricks; grandson, Ben; granddaughters Jeana and Diana; two great-grandsons, Perry and Kenny Schow.

WILLIAM THEODORE "BARNEY" RAPP, born March 31, 1920 in Newark, NJ. Graduated high school, entered the US Naval Academy in 1939 and commissioned an ensign June 19, 1942. In June 1942 he was attached to the Staff of Commander Amphibious Force, Atlantic Fleet; October 1942 served as Gunnery Division officer in USS *Ranger* (CV-4); January 1943 became Gunnery Division officer in USS *Princeton* (CVL-23). Just days prior to sailing on her last voyage he transferred off *Princeton* to flight training in November 1944-Oct. 1, 1945 with his designation as naval aviator.

Barney served in Patrol Squadrons 122 and 29 where he participated in Alaskan area deployments until September 1948. From March 1949 to December 1953 he served with the Bureau of Aeronautics, Los Angles office, Guided Missile School, Fort Bliss, TX and Operations Officer, NS Argentia, Newfoundland.

Following return to CONUS he served with Patrol Squadron 8 as operations officer and XO deploying to the Mediterranean, Puerto Rico and Argentina. After a tour at Naval Air Ordnance Test Station, Chincoteague, VA as OIC, Guided Missile Unit 11, he served as operations officer, XO and CO of VP-10 at NAS Brunswick, ME. Following this he served in USS *Valcour* (AVP-55) as XO, attended the Naval War College, Newport, RI and served in Bureau of Naval Weapons, Navy Department. He obtained a MA degree in international affairs from George Washington University.

His next tour was with the Navy Department as director of Programs and Budget Division Office of the Chief of Naval Material. From August 1964-65 served as CO of USS *Rankin* (AKA-103). During this time he was joined by his middle son, Ken, a Marine PFC deployed in USS *Boxer* (LPH-4), participating in Operation Steel Pike (October-November 1964) and the Dominican Republic incursion (April-June 1965). His next assignment was as faculty advisor at Armed Forces Staff College, Norfolk followed by Commander, Fleet Air Wing 3, NAS Brunswick, ME. He found himself back in Washington, DC as director Fleet Resources Office, HQ, Naval Materiel Command.

Promoted to rear admiral in June 1968, he reported to Okinawa as Commander Patrol Force, 7th Fleet/Command US Taiwan Patrol Force/Commander Fleet Air Wing 1. Then back to Washington, DC and the Naval Ship Systems Command where he served as deputy commander for Plans, Programs and Financial Management/Comptroller.

Upon his promotion to vice admiral August 1972, he was en route to Pearl Harbor as Commander Antisubmarine Warfare Force, US Pacific Fleet (COMASWFORPAC). This command was merged with that of Commander US First Fleet and reorganized. On Feb. 1, 1973 Adm. W.F. "Bull" Halsey's US Third Fleet was recommissioned with Rapp in command. This new command remained on Ford Island directly next to Battleship Row. He stayed with this command until retiring Sept. 1, 1974. Earned the Legion of Merit w/Gold Star, Navy Commendation Medal, Presidential Unit Citation Ribbon, Navy Unit Commendation Ribbon and numerous WWII and Vietnam Conflict medals.

Barney passed away Nov. 16, 1988 after a long illness. He is interred at Arlington National Cemetery. He left his wife, Cathy, three sons: Bill, Ken and Rick; five grandchildren and four great-grandchildren.

He was a life long New York Yankee fan who in the 1950s was known to sit in his Ford until late in the evening listening to them on the radio in spite of squadrons of mosquitoes attacking him. There is no doubt that he was Navy through and through. Only after cutting his finger did his kids learn that his blood was not Navy blue. He swore his oldest son Bill into the Navy; his youngest, Rick was NROTC candidate at UVA until medical complications forced him to resign; middle son, Ken almost left the fold by enlisting in the Marines. Barney never stopped growing. After retirement, he started his second career ... living and working for the Lord with the same determination he displayed for "his" Navy. His walk with the Lord and the love of and for his family sustained him to the end.

RICHARD E. RHOADES, born Nov. 7, 1925 in Winslow, AZ. Received BSME from Rice University and a BS in mining engineering from University of Arizona. He joined the USN on June 1, 1943 and was discharged June 18, 1946 as ensign.

He retired Dec. 31, 1990 as manager of Tyrone Open Pit Mine, Tyrone, NM. Married to June, he has five children: Richard, Charles, Carol, Mary Ann and David; and 10 grandchildren.

LOWELL D. RICHARDS, born Sept. 24, 1936 in De Smet, SD. Received a BA in 1962 from South Dakota State University; MA in 1964 from Vanderbilt University and MS in 1968 from Kansas State University.

Richards joined the South Dakota National Guard Dec. 23, 1953 and US Marine Corps Feb. 16, 1955. Served with Marine Detachment on USS *Princeton* 1955 to June 1957; 2nd Battalion Landing Team, 6th Marine Regt. Mediterranean Sea aboard the USS *Cambria* (APA-36) and the USS *Pocono* (AGC-16). Involved in the Beirut, Lebanon UN action. Discharged April 1, 1959 as sergeant.

He retired May 1998 from Office of Air, Rail and Transit, South Dakota Department of Transportation. Married to Judith, he has two children, Michael and Mark; four grandchildren: Thea, Olivia, Jackson and Gabriel.

JAMES G. RICHELIEU, born July 14, 1938 in Red Bluff, CA. Attended Chico State College for four years. He joined the USN on July 1, 1956. Served on two trips to Japan (where he climbed Mt. Fuji) in 1956 and 1958. Discharged July 14, 1959 as 2/c radar.

He is still working as a general building contractor. Married to Barbara, he has two sons, Dan and Steve.

HAROLD STEVE ROBERTSON, born March 16, 1945 in Whitfield County, Dalton, GA. He joined the USN on April 6, 1962. Served in Vietnam during 1963-65 and Subic Bay, Philippines. He recalls going to the aid of a sinking Japanese freighter damaged from a storm.

Discharged March 17, 1965 as E-3, he was awarded National Defense Service Medal and Vietnam Service Medal.

Current civilian employment: Battey Machiney.

LAWRENCE P. "PAT" ROMIG, born Dec. 2, 1940 in Whittier, CA. Graduated from high school and attended some college. He joined the USN in June 1958 and was discharged in September 1961 as E3. Current employment: Aerospace. Married to Patty, he has a son, Barry.

LAWRENCE RUBIN, born March 8, 1921 in Dayton, OH. At 3 years old his parents moved to Chicago, IL. It was at Great Lakes NTS, IL where he started his Navy career as a 3/c storekeeper on Dec. 22, 1941. From there he was sent to the Receiving Station, Pier 92 in New York. There the SS *Normandie* was being fitted for a troop ship and caught fire. He helped to fight the fire, then assigned to stand watch over her.

Next he was sent to Norfolk, VA where he was assigned to the USS *Wasp* aircraft carrier as storekeeper 3/c petty officer. At this time the USS *Wasp* was under British Admiralty. In April and May 1942 they assisted the British by bringing two loads of Spitfire fighters to Malta, making two trips through the Straits of Gibraltar to help save Malta. Then they went through the Panama Canal to the Pacific Ocean to the next battle area. After six months, in September 1942, the USS *Wasp* was sunk by three torpedoes off Guadalcanal. Servicemen with and without life jackets were in the ocean for three hours hanging on 2x4s and each other. Depth charges were going off all around them. A destroyer finally picked them up.

He was then sent to Pre-commissioning School to put the USS *Princeton* in commission at the Philadelphia Navy Yard Feb. 25, 1943. He was the first police petty officer of the S Division and also the last. He still has his badge. They were sent to the Pacific Coast. After their aircraft hit many islands held by the Japanese, a dive bomber exploded which caused their ship to catch fire. They sounded battle stations and the men tried to save the ship, but to no avail. They then had to abandon ship with a destroyer alongside to rescue them.

When he returned to the States, he sent for his girlfriend, Lorraine. They were married May 6, 1945 in San Francisco, CA by a Navy Chaplain. By his next assignment the war was over and he came home. Discharged at Great Lakes Sept. 13, 1945.

Before the war he had two years of college but decided to become an electrician. After 35 years in that career, he retired and has since volunteered at the Veteran's Hospital in Chicago. He now has 17,500 hours of service and is still going strong. Also, he has been asked to tell his experiences at neighborhood schools and they are in awe.

Lorraine and he, now married over 55 years, have three wonderful daughters and five grandchildren.

ARTHUR LEIF "SANDY" SANDERHOFF, born June 9, 1927 in Lake Forest, IL. Attended Spartan School of Aero Engineering and ROTC Fork Union Military Academy. He joined the USN in 1945 and the Air Force in 1951. Stationed on USS *Little Rock*, USS *Princeton*, NAS Norfolk, VA based; NAS Bolling, Washington, DC; Norfolk, VA; Quonset Point, RI; Enid AFB; Andrews AFB and Kelly AFB.

Memorable experiences: shipping escort on USS *Little Rock* to England; USS *Princeton* (CV-37) B-25 pilot in the US Air Force, special air mission. Discharged from the Navy in 1947 as aviation, machinist mate 3/c and from the USAF in 1957 as first lieutenant. Awarded American, European, WWII VM, Korean, Good Conduct Medal and Rifle Sharpshooter.

Retired as captain in 1985 from US Air after 30 years. Married to Lois, he has four children and two grandchildren.

LUCIANO R. "LOU" SHAFFER, born Nov. 18, 1923. He joined the USN in February 1943 and attended boot camp at Great Lakes. He did extensive training as an ordnance man in Oklahoma. Then went to Jacksonville, FL for training as an aircrew-man and gunner aboard PBYs. He then went back to Oklahoma for commando training for 10 weeks. He shipped out with two seabags, one Marine and the other Navy equipped with a Springfield rifle and about 150 rounds of ammo to Treasure Island, CA.

Boarded a Kaiser Liberty ship in January 1944 with 5,000 or so sailors, Marines and soldiers; 30 days later he arrived in Nomea, Caledonia. Two weeks later he was in Espartos Santos, New Hebrides and expecting to be shipped out to some island, because of the two seabags to defend and fly out as an aircrew-man and gunner. The next thing he knew, about five of the aircrew-men and other sailors were boarding the USS *Princeton*. His Marine seabag, rifle and ammo were taken and placed down in the hold. He and his other seabag were sent down to the fantail where his quarters were going to be. They were told they were going to be standby replacements for TBFs and Ms as gunners. So until they were needed, they worked with ordnance crew checking the 50 cal. and 30s aboard the TBFs; F-6Fs machine guns, loading bombs and torpedoes.

As time went on, the *Princeton* was involved in seven or eight conflicts until the final one of second Philippines Sea Battle. On the morning of Oct. 24, 1944, he was working on F-6F wing guns. They were in a squall and the planes were wet. He was standing on the tire holding on to the folded wing when he slipped and started to slide off the tire. His left hand holding the wing as he slid, cut his forefinger to the bone. He went to the First Aid Station under the forward deck to have it stitched when the 20s began to fire and the whole ship shook when the bomb hit. The doctor must have put three yards of gauze on his finger. He got up topside and smoke was billowing out the center of the ship. His shipmates were trying to battle the flames, but no water.

Next thing he knew they were pushing planes off the side. The destroyers came alongside to help fight the fires; then the rear elevator blew up. Soon afterwards, they got the word to abandon ship. All of them were topside of flight deck clamored down to the bow. There his boot camp training came in, he took off his shoes, inflated his life vest by mouth and began to climb down hand over hand on the line hanging there.

He entered the water, swam on his back until he was far enough away from the ship and floated for a couple of hours until the destroyer *Irwin* picked him up. He stayed on the *Irwin*, even after three torpedo gyros were fouled up and came back at them. They reached Hawaii and then went to the States for a 30-day survivors leave. He put the rest of his time in Pensacola, FL as an aircraft gunnery instructor on Liberator bombers. Sent to Toledo, OH to be discharged March 27, 1944. He was and still is very proud to have been a member of the USS *Princeton* crew.

He was employed with Stewart Enterprises part-time and retired from Hunter Dodge in 1991. Married to Sally (deceased in 2001), he has a daughter Antoinette and granddaughter Amanda.

BOB J. SIEBRASSE, born June 29, 1925 in Big Sandy, MT. Received a BS in 1950 and MS in 1956 from Montana State College. He joined the USN in March 23, 1944. Served in Navy Armed Guard, SS *Christopher L. Sholes,* liberty ship; tanker, delivered diesel fuel to Oran, North Africa; Sicily and Napoli, Italy; SS *George H. Dern*, liberty ship and USS *Princeton* (CV-37). Discharged June 1946 as RM 3/c. He passed the test for RM 2/c last time at sea, but doesn't know if it was turned in.

Retired in 1981 as associate professor at Northern Montana College. Married to Sarah, he has four children: Patricia, John, Paul and Tim; five grandchildren: Greg, Sarah, Lindsey, Breanna and Brynn.

EMIL V. SMYER, born July 5, 1921 in Drake County, OH. Received a BSc in agronomy from Washington State University in 1951. A naval

aviator, he flew off carriers in WWII and flew transports in Korean War. He was aboard the *Princeton* when it was commissioned and for shakedown cruise. Later went through the Panama Canal aboard the *Princeton*. Discharged as a full lieutenant.

Retired after 30 years July 5, 1981 as a captain for Trans World Airlines on his 60th birthday. Married to Ann, he has two daughters, Stephanie in Seattle, WA and Susan in San Diego, CA.

GARY F. STANEART, born Nov. 15, 1941. Graduated high school and joined the US Marine Corps on Jan. 3, 1961. He was discharged with rank of corporal Dec. 15, 1964. Employed with Verizon, he is married to Vonnie; has three daughters and three grandchildren.

WALTER CHARLES STRENK, born Jan. 23, 1917 in Corona, FL. Graduated from Hazelton High School, Hazelton, PA in 1935. He joined the Navy in August 1936. Served overseas in Bermuda, Panama and Cuba. Sea duty included tours aboard the USS *Texas*, USS *Wyoming*, USS *Mississippi*, USS *Jason* (AR-8), USS *Monterey Bay* (CVL-26) and the USS *Thetis* Bay (CVHA-1). He was a plankowner aboard the USS *Princeton* serving aboard from July 1945 to October 1948.

After retirement from the Navy he was employed by Pacific Architects and Engineers and worked on various Air Force bases in Thailand from 1967-75. While there he was made an honorary member of the Green Berets by the 46th Special Forces Co. (Airborne), 1st Special Forces in Thailand. Retired January 1967 as commissioned warrant officer CWO-4 after serving 30 years.

He retired from Pacific Architects and Engineers in 1975. Married Anna Kutz Sept. 25, 1948 in Coronado, CA and had one son, Andrew. Walter C. Strenk passed away April 23, 2001.

HIRAM S. TEMPLE, born Feb. 8, 1926 in Hawthorne, NJ. He joined the USN Jan. 28, 1944 and served on the USS *Princeton* (CVL-23). A plane handler in the V1 Division aboard USS *Princeton* (CVL-23), his battle station was on the flight deck. He saw the bomb dropped by the Japanese "Judy" bomber coming down toward the flight deck and hit the deck. When the bomb exploded several decks below, it shook him up and down. He helped push planes over the side and manned a hose to fight the fires raging on the hangar deck, but couldn't get any water pressure. He could not get to his life jacket when the order was passed to abandon ship, so he made his way to the bow of the ship and slid down the chain net to the anchor. Just about the time he entered the water a wave carried him between the rescue ship USS *Irwin* (DD-794) and the *Princeton*. After making several attempts to climb the rope net, he fell back into the sea. Two sailors from the *Irwin* hollered, "Hang on." Both climbed down and pulled him up and pumped water out of him. He owes them his life, he doesn't know their names, but thanks to them he has been able to lead a good life. He wants to thank the two men and everyone else that participated in the *Princeton's* rescue. Discharged Oct. 29, 1946 as seaman 1/c and awarded APCM w/3 stars, Philippine Liberation w/star, American Area and WWII VM.

He retired Feb. 8, 1981 after 36 years with the US Post Office. Married over 55 years to Elsie, he has four children: Mary Ruth, Carrol, Lester and Tina; eight grandchildren, 12 great-grandchildren and two great-great-grandchildren.

BILL ARLIN THORNTON, born June 1, 1934 in LaJunta, CO. Graduated from Swink High School, Swink, CO. He joined the service Dec. 11,

1953 and served on the USS *Princeton* and USS *Essex*. Participated in the evacuation of the Tachens, February 1955 and became a shellback July 1957. He received an honorable discharge as EM1 and was discharged from the Reserves Dec. 10, 1961.

Retired in July 1989 after 38 years working for Santa Fe Railway in Colorado, New Mexico, Illinois and Kansas. He married Helen Fink on July 18, 1958 in Canon City, CO and has three children; Joe, Pam and Vicki; 11 grandchildren.

EDWARD W. TOLMAN, born July 13, 1930 in Bucksport, ME. Attended one year of business college. He joined the USN in 1950 and served in Korea. One of his memorable experiences was watching the planes taking off and coming back from their missions. Discharged in 1954 as FN.

He retired Dec. 15, 1922 from Boeing Co. Married To Gwendolyn, he has four children: Edward, Lonnie, Mark and Aaron; four grandchildren: Jhade Tolman, Jason and Nathan Lian and Sara Potter; three step-grandchildren: Gerrick, Mason and Preston Howard; and one great-grandchild Stephon Faust.

EDWARD JOHN VANDENBERG, born May 26, 1916 in Grand Rapids, MI. Graduated from University of Michigan, Ann Arbor, MI, Class of 1938. He volunteered for the USN; commissioned and ordered to Washington, DC in 1942. In 1943 he was sent to Subchaser School in Florida and received orders to the USS *Princeton*.

He and Mary Booth Francis were married in November 1943 and he proceeded to the West Coast for transportation to the *Princeton*. Joined the ship December 1943. Lt. Edward Vandenberg was lost when the *Princeton* was sunk on Oct. 24, 1944 in the Battle of Leyte Gulf.

GILBERT W. VATTER, born Oct. 10, 1927 in Lancaster, PA. Received a BA in German from Franklin & Marshall College in 1953. Joined the USN Sept. 17, 1945 and served on the USS *Princeton* (CV-37) Dec. 17, 1945 in Cuba, Trinidad, Panama Canal, Manila, PI; Yokosuka, Japan; Sasebo, Japan; Tsingtao, China; Shanghai, China; Kwajalein, Marshall Islands and Hawaii.

He recalls the 21 gun salute as President Truman reviewed the Eighth Atlantic Fleet; the body of Manuel Quezon (ex-Philippine president) was brought aboard, Task Force 38 maneuvers and the full dressed ship on Chilean Independence Day. Discharged Sept. 28, 1948 as QM2.

Retired in 1992 after 40 years in the clock/watch industry as vice-president of Seiko Corporation. Married Patricia Gehman in 1953 and has two daughters, Carol Vatter and Julia Tibbett; two grandsons, Kirkham and Liam Tibbett.

RICHARD MICHAEL VITTETOE, born Oct. 23, 1925 in Keota, IA. Graduated eighth grade from St. Elizabeth's School, Harper, IA. He joined the USN Jan. 21, 1944 and reported to Farragut, ID, Camp Benyon, Co. 128. Embarked from Shumaker, CA on a transport ship to Pearl Harbor and taken on a PT boat to the USS *Princeton*. The USS *Princeton* headed to the South Pacific Theater, engaging in Battles of Guam, Saipan and Philippines in 1944.

His memorable experience was Oct. 24, 1944, the day the USS *Princeton* was crippled by a Japanese aircraft; the abandonment, sinking and surviving at sea. Honorably discharged as seaman 1/c. Earned three Bronze Battle Stars and one Silver Survivor Star.

He is owner/operator of the family grain farm. Married to Ardyce Fay Wavrin, he has five daughters: Cheryl Lee Barnett, Mary Sue Ruggles, Fay Ann Vittetoe, Deborah Joan Adrian and Tina Maria Bullington; seven grandchildren: Christina Yochum, Scott Ruggles, Anthony and Tina Adrian; Veronica, Justin and Jacquelin Myer; two great-grandchildren, Logan Yochum and Lauren Ruggles.

JOHN WAYNE WATKINS, born Jan. 10, 1938 in Coleman, TX. He joined the USN June 20, 1955 and obtained his GED while in the service. Served on the Far Eastern Cruise and left San Diego Jan. 5, 1956. Sailed to Hawaii, Bangkok, Thailand; Yokosuka, Japan; Manila, PI; Subic Bay, PI; Okinawa; Kure, Japan; Keelung, Formosa; Sasebo, Japan; Hong Kong, BCC then homeward bound Aug. 1, 1956.

During the cruise the *Princeton* served as flagship for Carrier Division 17 and as floating airfield for Air Anti-submarine Squadrons 20 and 21 (combined into VS-21 on June 1) and Helicopter Anti-submarine Squadron 2, Detachment Nan (commissioned HS-6 June 1). With these units they became the center of a large operating force known as a Hunter-killer Task Group. Their mission was both simple and essential, "to seek out and destroy their deadly underwater enemy, the submarine." This was known as Operation Firmlink off Formosa.

He remembers vividly that the temperature on the ship was 120 degrees round the clock, no air conditioning. Everybody had Chinese Jungle Rot. The only thing sick bay had was a fungicide ointment and it didn't work. The only thing for relief was scratch until it bled. They also had a problem with crabs. Hadn't been in contact with a supply ship, therefore, no crab powder. In the entire R Division one other shipmate and himself did not have crabs. He doesn't know what happened to the other guy, but he had advanced to a top rack and during off duty hours his shipmates would try to put crabs in the rack with him. There was a beam over his head where he kept a dog wrench. It didn't take many busted knuckles from that dog wrench to convince his fellow shipmates in R division that they were not going to give him the crabs. One shipmate threatened to shave a trail down the middle, set fire to one side and stab them with an ice pick when they ran across.

If Harvey Goss is still around, Watkins still wants to go grizzly bear hunting in Montana and wants a spaghetti dinner at Louis Cavalieres mother's house in southern California. He was discharged in June 1963 as DC3.

Retired Jan. 10, 1993 from Texas Department MHMR. Married to Elois, he has a son, Allen Wayne and three grandchildren.

HARRY JAMES WHEELER, born May 24, 1946 in Prince George County, MD. Obtained an AS in fire science from Mt. San Jacinto College, California in 1977. He joined the USN and served on the USS Princeton (LPH-5) Jan. 26, 1965. Participated in operations Jackstay, Osage, Deckhouse I, Nathan Hale, Deckhouse II and Hastings.

He was separated Dec. 17, 1967 in Long Beach, CA. Enlisted in the Nevada Air National Guard Sept. 30, 1980 and retired Dec. 31, 2000 as master sergeant (E-7) NVANG. He attended a ships reunion of the USS *Princeton* (CVL-23/CV-37/LPH-5) July 1, 2000 in Seattle, WA. After 30 years seven of them reunited with war stories and experiences: James Love Sr., Garry Myrick, Dayton D. "JR" Pierce, Andy Chisolm, Henry Bethel and Michael Huckalsay.

He was employed with Truckee Meadows Fire Protection District, Washoe, County, NV July 1979-July 2000; he now works for the city of Reno Fire Department, Reno, NV.

Married to Jo Ann McKinney, he has three children: Harry, Rebecca and Amy; four grandchildren: Haley, Makeala and Hunter Wheeler and Gabriel Wheeler-Hammond.

JOHN A. WILLIAMS, born Oct. 27, 1922 in Kalamazoo, MI. Attended junior college four years. He joined the USN Dec. 22, 1941. Served on the USS *Hornet* (CV-8) which sank Oct. 26, 1942 and the *Princeton* (CVL-23) which sank Oct. 23, 1944 in Leyte Gulf. He was a plank member of the USS *Princeton*, fire controlman 2/c, 5th Div. His job was to keep the 40mm guns synchronized with the Mark 52 director. They had problems when a plane missed the tailhook and landed in the gun mount. They worked all night, put new gun barrels in, repaired the hydraulics and had to synchronize the gun with the synchos on the director.

It is a sad feeling when they go over the side and abandon ship. It's their home and everything they own is lost. They still have their heart and soul to survive. His last tour of duty was as a fire control instructor at Pacific Beach, San Diego on five-inch 38, 40mm Mark 37 director, 57 and 63 directors. Discharged from the Navy Sept. 27, 1945 and from the Reserves October 1950 as FC 1/c.

He retired February 1985 from General Motors. Married to Bea, he has three children, seven grandchildren and five great-grandchildren.

CLAUDE F. WITZELING, born Aug. 31, 1933 in Wausau, WI. Enlisted May 13, 1953 and traveled to Great Lakes NTC. In late fall of 1953 he transferred to Norfolk, VA to wait for the USS *Roosevelt* to return from the Mediterranean tour of duty. He boarded the *Roosevelt* to sail from Norfolk to Bremerton, WA. Because the ship was so large they could not go through the Panama Canal and had to go around the Horn of South America. Going to Rio De Janeiro they crossed the equator and were initiated as shellbacks. He carried a card for the rest of his naval career as a horned shellback.

They took the *Roosevelt* into Bremerton to be put into dry-dock and fitted with a canted flight deck. It was one of the earliest carriers to have this done. With his type of deck they were able to launch and recover aircraft at the same time. From Bremerton he went aboard the USS *Princeton* May 1954 at San Diego and received orders for Fire Control School. In January 1956 they left for the Far East, stopped in Hawaii and then on to Japan. Spent eight months training on Princeton (CVS-37) in Japan, Thailand, Hong Kong, Okinawa and the Philippines. Returned to San Diego August 1956 and discharged May 12, 1957 as FT2.

He retired Dec. 31, 1997 as owner of Modern Builders & Suppliers, Inc. in Wausau, WI. Married Jean April 1954 and the best years of their life were spent in San Diego in 1954-55.

He has two sons, one daughter, two grandsons and two granddaughters.

JOSEPH P. WORK, born Aug. 30, 1931 in Spangler, PA. Graduated from Penn State University and Dickinson School of Law JD. He joined the USN in August 1949. Served in the Western Pacific, Sea of Japan and Korean waters; two tours (1950-51 and 1951-52).

The whole time he was on that great ship, starting with Capt. Bill Gallery and continuing through two other commanding officers, was all a great experience, all memorable and an exciting couple of years. He returned to the Fleet Airborne Radar School on North Island and remained there until his discharge May 3, 1953 as an ET3.

He has spent the last 27 years of his career as a Federal AL Judge from which he retired Jan. 6, 1996.

Married to Joanne Kauczka for over 32 years, he has five children, three grandchildren and one great-grandchild.

JERRY W. ZENTZ, born Oct. 15, 1934 in Poplar, MN. Graduated from Clarkston High School, Clarkston, WA. He joined the USN in Aug. 28, 1952. Served aboard the USS *Noxubee* (AOG-56), USS *Aucilla* (AO-56), Norfolk Group Reserve Fleet, USS *DeHaven* (DD-727), USS *Princeton* (CVS-37), Aug. 2, 1957-Dec. 16, 1958; USS *Hornet* (CVA-42), CINCLANTFLT HQ and USS *FDR* (CVA-42). Discharged April 2, 1962 as ET1 and had been notified he had been selected to be promoted to ETC.

In December 1957 heavy rains on the island of Ceylon destroyed 10,000 homes. In January 1958 the *Princeton* delivered 400,000 pounds of emergency food supplies and 3,000 pounds of medical supplies to the devastated area. Anchored in Colombo for liberty and 3,000 people toured the ship. They received a "well done" from the President as well as CNO, Admiral Burke. During the exercise they became shellbacks. He still remembers kissing the Royal Baby's belly.

After leaving the Navy he worked for Boeing for about 14 months; Tally Corp. for five years and retired after 26 years from Intermec in 1995. Sold their house and traveled in a RV around the US for two years and now live north of Spokane, WA.

Married to Marlene Anderson for over 45 years, he has four children: David, Tim, Julia Buckner and Sharon Guernsey; 10 grandchildren: Michael, Aaron, Jennifer, Lydia, Erica, Andrea, Alex, Tarah, Tyler and TJ.

INDEX

A
Apollo 10 42, 43, 44, 45, 46, 48
Apollo 11 12, 42
Apra Harbor, Guam 3

B
Bell, Norman 57
Bishop 48
Bishop, Ronald 41
Boling, Gordon 41, 42
Bollinger, Harold 63
Bolton 60
Brachmonte 60
Brest, Graham 63
Brookhart, Dick 63
Brooks, Joe 27
Bruny, David 61
Buckman, Ed 28, 29
Buelow, Fred 39
Buracker 23

C
Carcione, Frank 26
Carius, Robert 42, 43, 44, 45, 46, 47, 48, 49, 51, 52, 53, 55
Cartmell, Gary 41, 42
Cavanaugh 60
Cernan, Eugene 42, 43, 46, 47
Chaput, A.L. 13
Chittom, C.D. 59
Coffey, Charles 58
Cole, James Richard 40
Colern, Richard 17, 56, 59, 60, 62
Collett 17
Cooper, J.R. 59
Cooper, Paul L. 30
Craig, Clem 29
Creek, James 3, 59, 60
Crosby, Clayton B. 40
Cruse, Carl 46, 47
Custer, David 41

D
de Saussure 49
DeLand, R.B. 14
Dickerson, R.L. 26
Dodds, Mrs. Harold 6, 9
Douglas, J.W. 59
Dunlap, H.E. 25

F
Fahan, Robert 58, 61, 63
Frazier, Donald 33
Fugaro, A.M. 26

G
Gallery, William O. 34
Gamblin, Harold 69
Garber, Jan 25
Gary, Raymond 63
Geer, Don 36
George, Gordon 33
Godwin, W.B. 59
Gowen, G.A. 49
Gray, David 31, 35, 36
Gregg 32
Gregg, Jack 58
Grisamore 60

H
Hansson, Herbert 36
Harrison, William 32
Hausler, Randall 41
Havana Harbor 13
Hawkins, Horace 32
Henderson, George R. 6, 18
Herbert, Leo 62, 63
Herbert, Martin 57, 58, 60, 61, 62, 63
Hickman, William 32
Holliday, Kate 35
Hopkins, Charles 26
Hoskens 25
Hoskins 23
Hoskins, John M. 9
House, R.M. 57, 58
Huber 60
Hughes, F. Massie 60

I
Irwin 8, 9, 22, 23

J
Jackson, Richard M. 20
Jones, Don 43
Jurgens, Dick 25

K
Kagy, R.E. 69
Keester, Larry 57
Keith, Gail 63
Kelly, Donald F. 25
Kenton, Stan 25
Killingsworth 33
Klaus, Bob 30
Kolar, George 62, 63

L

Lawrence, Richard 14
Leichy 60
Lopez, Manuel 26
Lunt, W.K. 41
Lynam, John 26

M

MacArthur 23
Mack, Leroy 29
Martin 42
Martin, Frank 33
McBurney, Bill 35, 38
McCain Jr, John S. 48
McKinnon, Dan 47
McRae, E.W. 57, 58, 59
Michalek 37
Mirasola, P. 26
Moody, John 33
Morrison 9
Mullen 60
Muse 11

N

Neece, Gerry 57, 61
Nemerovsky, Jerry 62

O

Ogilvie, Jack 63
Okinawa 11

P

Parsons, Seymour 18
Peers, Ronald 58
Petrillo 25
Pioneer 11
Porphy, J.R. 26
Puryear, J.M. 59

Q

Queson, Manuel 9

R

Radford, Arthur W. 18
Rapp, K.S. 61
Respess, Tom 54, 55
Richards, Lowell D. 38, 39

S

Saggs, J.R. 59
Sanderhoff, A. Leif 24, 32
Sanders 60
Sandifer, C.F. 69
Sasebo 29
Scarsheim, H.V. 29
Schroder 56
Seipel 60
Sheik 11
Shenkenburger 60
Shoup, J.C. 69
Siebrasse, Bob J. 24
Smith, Dallas 58
Smith, J.V. 48
Stafford 43, 44, 46, 47
Stafford, Thomas 42
Stebbins, Harry 18
Stephens 51, 52, 55
Stephens, Franklin 49, 54
Stiles, Ralph 25
Streble, Carl 58
Stullken, Don 43, 46

T

Talley 17, 56
Tiger Balm Garden, Hong Kong 60
Tom 60
Tupts, Charles 36

U

USNS *Weigel* 31, 32
USS *Arizona* 40
USS *Arlington* 44
USS *Bennington* 41
USS *Birmingham* 7, 8, 9, 19, 20, 22
USS *Bon Homme Richard* 32
USS *Boxer* 31, 32, 33
USS *Carpenter* 44
USS *Chipola* 44
USS *Essex* 31, 33
USS *Lexington* 67
USS *Maine* 25
USS *Monterey* 31
USS *Morrison* 20
USS *Reno* 6, 8, 9
USS *Small* 49
USS *Strauss* 49
USS *Walke* 33
USS *Yorktown* 66

V

Vatter, Gilbert 25, 26
Vittetoe, Fay A. 18
Vittetoe, Richard M. 18
Vitzthum, John 58

W

Walstrom, Dick 58
Ward, Robert 49
Wilson, George 36
Witt, K.W. 26
Wright 60

Y

Yokosuku, Japan 58
Young 46, 47
Young, John 42, 43

www.ingramcontent.com/pod-product-compliance
Lightning Source LLC
Chambersburg PA
CBHW061207230426
43664CB00030B/2943